The SCIENCE *of* SOCIAL INTELLIGENCE

The SCIENCE of SOCIAL INTELLIGENCE

BE MAGNETIC, MAKE AN IMPRESSION AND WIN FRIENDS

Patrick King

Published by
Rupa Publications India Pvt. Ltd 2022
7/16, Ansari Road, Daryaganj
New Delhi 110002

Sales centres:
Allahabad Bengaluru Chennai
Hyderabad Jaipur Kathmandu
Kolkata Mumbai

Copyright © PKCS Media, Inc 2022

Published under arrangement with PKCS
Media, Inc. through TLL Literacy Agency

All rights reserved.
No part of this publication may be reproduced, transmitted,
or stored in a retrieval system, in any form or by any means,
electronic, mechanical, photocopying, recording or otherwise,
without the prior permission of the publisher.

The views and opinions expressed in this book are the author's own and
the facts are as reported by him which have been verified to the extent
possible, and the publishers are not in any way liable for the same.

P-ISBN-978-93-5520-829-3
E-ISBN-978-93-5520-830-9

First impression 2022

10 9 8 7 6 5 4 3 2 1

Printed in India

This book is sold subject to the condition that it shall not,
by way of trade or otherwise, be lent, resold, hired out, or otherwise
circulated, without the publisher's prior consent, in any form of
binding or cover other than that in which it is published.

Table of Contents

Introduction 7

Chapter 1. The Social Animal 11

Chapter 2. Become a "Cool Kid" 27

Chapter 3. The Value of Shutting Up 43

Chapter 4. Just Be Positive? Really? 59

Chapter 5. Perception Part One 75

Chapter 6. Perception Part Two 93

Chapter 7. A Simple Roadmap 115

Chapter 8. Emotional Calibration 133

Chapter 9. Traits for Social Catastrophe 151

Chapter 10. The Interconnected World 167

Chapter 11. Social Efficiency (Who to Spend Time and Effort On) 185

Conclusion 201

Speaking and Coaching 205

Cheat Sheet 207

Introduction

Years ago (longer than I would like to admit), I was an emotionally anguished teenager. Par for the course, really.

One day, the fragile bundle of emotion that was me came to a peak when I encountered a cashier who I thought had been rude to me for weeks. Our normal conversations went something like, "I'll have the salmon bagel." "Is that all?" "Yes, thank you." "Okay, that will be three dollars."

Can you feel her contempt for me?

Of course not. I had made it up in my mind when I decided to be offended at anyone and everything. But what's important is that I believed the story I had created for myself. In doing so, I started to treat this poor cashier like she was the scum of the Earth to get even with her, and she actually started becoming rude to me. Keep in mind she was a cashier, so she was literally paid to be nice to people, and she had started to speak rudely to me. I must have been a terribly annoying teenager.

I had created a story in my mind, acted on it, and brought it to reality in the worst of ways. I didn't realize until far later that this was the Pygmalion Effect at work, which states that, however you treat someone, that's the person they will become to you. If you treat someone as if they are kind and magnanimous, you will probably encourage that side of them. You'll be generous and caring to them. However, if you treat someone as if they are swine, you won't give them a chance to shine and you will bring out their worst sides—and that's exactly how I was with this poor cashier.

That was my first peek into how small things can dramatically make you more likable, charismatic, or the complete opposite. It was a whole new understanding of social intelligence and what it takes to succeed with people. It's not necessarily just knowing the best small-talk topics or being able to make powerful eye contact as magazines and blog articles would have you believe.

We make the vast majority of our decisions underneath the surface of our conscious thinking. This is terrifying if you don't know what the decisions are being made on, but that's where this book comes in. The goal here is to impart understanding of what people are really looking for when they judge and evaluate people. Some of it will be nearly common sense, while some of it will be completely counterintuitive.

We are ruled by our brains, and our social lives and relationships depend on decoding it! You are about to embark on a journey into the depths of your mind and what gives you the feeling of chemistry with one person, and what gives you the worst feeling of all with another: complete apathy and instant forgetting.

Along the way, you'll learn more about Pygmalion, with dozens of other studies from biological science, social psychology, and even behavioral economics. Underneath, we are all wired with the same hardware. Our software is a little different, but our core drives and motivations are just about standardized. Again, this can be terrifying—but hopefully, after the end of this book, you see more opportunity than chances to stumble socially.

Social intelligence and understanding the relationships that surround us are key to getting what you want in life. Science and research have shown us a way to predictably deal with that which is theoretically the most unpredictable: people.

Chapter 1. The Social Animal

Human beings are, both from a biological and evolutionary standpoint, social animals. Regardless of where an individual may fall on the spectrum of introversion and extroversion, some amount of social interaction is simply an integral part of life. It's something we want and also something we need.

Over two millennia ago, the famous philosopher Aristotle was quoted as saying, "Society is something that precedes the individual. Anyone who either cannot lead the common life or is so self-sufficient as not to need to, and therefore does not partake of society, is either a beast or a god." The ability of our species to communicate with each other more effectively than any other species on Earth is the predominant factor that propelled us to the top of the food chain. And as civilization advances, social skills have remained a very important part of what makes people successful as individuals. If you don't understand the science of social intelligence, you won't only be left behind; you'll be tragically unhappy.

The Effects of Loneliness

Social status and success are not mere matters of vanity or self-confidence, but rather crucial factors in our overall well-being. In fact, a lack of adequate social interaction or exposure can have very real consequences on our health, to the extent that loneliness can quite literally kill us.

The UCLA Loneliness Scale, a standard American questionnaire on loneliness, uses 20 questions to determine how often individuals experience feelings of close connection with others. The results indicated that as much as 30% of the total American population feels socially isolated and lonely at any given time.

That 30% figure is staggering when considering the implications of such loneliness on the health of some 95 million plus Americans. Loneliness varies widely with age but is especially detrimental for the elderly, as it can expedite the process of declining faculties and thus lead to earlier loss of life.

Naturally, you might be thinking that loneliness is a significantly bigger problem among elderly than the rest of the population because the members of an elderly person's social circle are more likely to have passed away as they all age. But it turns out that loneliness is also pervasive among middle-aged and young people.

A 2010 survey published by the AARP showed that greater than 33% of adults aged 45 and over report being chronically lonely, meaning that the feelings of loneliness have been consistent over a long period of time. This is even more alarming when you consider that when the same survey was conducted in 2000, only 20% of participants reported chronic loneliness. As approximately 10,000 Baby Boomers retire every day, that number is likely to grow considerably higher by 2020.

Researchers at the University of Chicago conducted a study over a five-year time frame that measured the correlation between loneliness and future depression. They found that people who had reported being lonely at the beginning of the study had a much greater tendency to report depression near the end of the study. In fact, the study found something truly surprising—people who reported loneliness at the beginning of the study were actually more likely to report feeling depressed at the end of the study than those who had reported being depressed to begin with. In other words, loneliness was a more common precedent for depression than actual depression was, and it's only getting worse.

This field of study will only continue to become more interesting as social media becomes a more significant part of our social lives. Many studies have already shown that high social media use has a negative effect on happiness and social fulfillment. At this point, social networks have grown too big to simply be phased out, so society will have to find ways to use those networks in more positive ways if loneliness and depression are to be curbed before reaching epidemic levels—if they haven't already.

The Social Brain Hypothesis

There is an evolutionary theory, known as the social brain hypothesis, which states that human brains evolved and became bigger in order to be more social, not the other way around. Furthermore, the theory states that increasing the capacity for communication about a wide range of subjects was the only reason that brains grew.

A British professor of anthropology and evolutionary psychology, Robin Dunbar, developed the theory as he learned from his studies that the size of a species' social group was the most accurate predictor of brain size—specifically, the outermost brain layer known as the neocortex.

Scientists believe that the first species with brains on the scale of modern humans— known as *Homo heidelbergenesis*—originally appeared some 600,000 to 700,000 years ago in Africa. These ancestors to *Homo sapiens* are also thought to be the first hominids who buried their dead, built central campsites, and utilized a division of labor where they worked together to hunt more effectively. This is no coincidence.

The reasoning behind the social brain hypothesis is that primates have unusually large brains for their body sizes relative to all other vertebrates—a result of needing to manage unusually complex social systems. In other words, in order for society to grow and thrive, the brain needed to evolve to be able to cope with the cognitive demands of being social.

As complex social behaviors limit the sizes of our social groups, there is emerging evidence that shows that the evolutionary process has favored individuals with the brain architecture most suited to performing and further developing those social behaviors. Interestingly, the main factor that distinguishes human brains from those of other primates is the size of the aforementioned neocortex—the part of the brain compromising many of the brain areas involved in complex social cognition. These functions include conscious thought, language, behavioral and emotional regulation, as well as empathy and the theory of mind—the thing that enables humans to understand the feelings and intentions of others.

What does all of this mean?

Humans, as a species, are endowed with a "social brain," which essentially biologically hard-wires us to interact with each other. Living a life of isolation is correlated with higher risk of loneliness and depression because it is fighting 600,000–700,000 years of evolution compelling us to socialize. We need to be around others for our mental health, no matter our temperament or personality type.

Brain structure and functionality change over thousands of years, and a large percentage of our modern communication methods are simply too new to be fully understood in relation to the social brain. The telephone has been around for just over a century, and instant messaging or texting for far less time than that. Is it possible that communicating predominantly through computers and phones instead of face to face simply doesn't fill our evolved need for socializing?

Or is it perhaps the rise in loneliness and feelings of isolation isn't a direct result of social networks and instant messaging, but rather an effect of not understanding how to use that technology in healthy ways?

In the meantime, it's important for all of us to observe how various levels of technology and specifically social media use impact our health and emotional well-being. If chronic loneliness ever becomes an issue for you, consider that perhaps you are not getting enough face-to-face interaction to meet your biological and evolutionary needs for sociality.

The Limits of Our Sociality

While social interaction has been the driving force behind the evolution of our brains, we do still have limits on how much socializing we can handle. Even the most extroverted person in the world has a finite amount of brain power and energy to socialize, meaning that we simply aren't capable of socializing forever or with everyone.

Robin Dunbar, the same scientist responsible for the social brain hypothesis, consulted the anthropological record in search of what was eventually named Dunbar's number—the cognitive limit to the number of people with whom it's possible for an individual to maintain stable social relationships. In this case, relationships are classified as stable when the given individual knows who every other individual is and how they relate to each of the other members of the group.

Dunbar proposed that an average human can comfortably maintain only about 150 stable relationships at any given time. Makes you rethink the number of people you are connected to on social media, doesn't it?

The number 150 isn't actually considered precise for all humans, but rather the average of the spectrum of possibilities for stable relationships that ranges from 100 to 200. It's generally thought that going too far over 200 will become unstable unless it is countered by the implementation of more restrictive rules, laws, and enforced norms. This number also doesn't include past social relationships that are no longer active or short-term acquaintances.

But how did Dunbar come to land on 150 people?

Well, he started off with the assumption that the current size of the average human neocortex became standard sometime around 250,000 years ago, during the Pleistocene epoch. Dunbar then went on to search anthropological and ethnographical literature looking for census-like information for various hunter-gather societies, hoping to find an accurate approximation of typical group sizes in those ancient societies. He found many examples of groups approximately 150 members large—from Neolithic farming villages and typical units of professional armies in Roman antiquity before the common era, all the way through time to modern Hutterite settlements originating in the 16th century.

Dunbar noted that ancient societies could be broken up into three categories based on group sizes: small bands of 30–50 people, cultural lineage groups of 100–200 people, and tribes with anywhere between 500 and 2500 members.

But 150 remained the most useful number, as a series of other values for modern human social capabilities were derived from it. There is actually a formula for roughly estimating all of the other numbers in the series, a "rule of three."

Multiplying the Dunbar number by three gives us an approximation of our total number of acquaintances, and multiplying that number by three again provides the absolute limit on our social relationships—the number of people for whom we can put a name to a face at a given time.

Dividing 150 by three, meanwhile, gives us the 50 friends whom we are at least somewhat close with. Doing so again will then give us our 15–20 confidants—the friends whom we can turn to for sympathy and support. Finally, dividing by three once more approximately gives us our most intimate friends or family members, the people who have the strongest influence on our personalities. It's a very real illustration of whom you should focus your attention and time on—and why to not spread yourself too thin.

While the compositions of all of these groups in the series are fluid, the overall size generally remains static. People might be moving from one level to another—or out of your social periphery altogether—but each void in your personal social hierarchy will be filled by someone new.

We often don't realize how systematic our social relationships are without thinking about them, but reflecting on the Dunbar numbers and how they relate to you personally can be quite revealing. Imagine you have a friend group with eight members, and you all hang out with each other on a regular basis. Regardless of how much you like each member of the group, it's practically certain that only a few of the group members are your best friends and confidants. It's great to have a big and diverse group, but there's just no getting around the fact that you have limited social energy and cognition.

One of the ways that being mindful about social limitations can help you is when it comes to jealousy. Given how important social status and success are to humans, it's not surprising that we can feel jealous about how friends, as well as romantic partners, choose to spend their time and social resources when it's not according to our wishes. Our neocortices aren't going to start growing again anytime soon, though, so the healthier route is to understand and accept that every person has a right to allocate their limited energy and cognition however they see fit. We can only control our own choices and decisions, and having expectations about what other people do doesn't make us any happier or healthier.

At the same time, it can be difficult for many of us to spend our own time in the ways we actually want to. The series of Dunbar's numbers seem to support the idea of having the highest quality relationships possible over a high quantity of them. Ultimately, we all have limits on how many close relationships we can maintain at a given time, and with that in mind, it certainly makes sense to pick our friends carefully and spend our time how we really want to. We are social creatures, to an extent.

Socializing, regardless of how you feel about it, is a fundamental part of being human. It was the driving force behind the evolution and growth of our brains—the thing that enabled us to create modern civilization as we know it today. Technology has now connected us to more people and across greater distances than ever before, yet loneliness and depression are on the rise. It will be up to each of us as individuals, therefore, to learn healthy social practices to adapt to our rapidly changing environments.

But as our technology continues to change, our brains still remain much the same as they have been for hundreds of thousands of years. Therefore, there is perhaps no better method to adapt your social skills to the modern day than to understand the fundamentals of social intelligence—to know which behaviors lead to isolation and depression, and which ones can improve your social satisfaction and fulfillment.

Chapter 2. Become a "Cool Kid"

There are no greater demonstrations of the importance of social status than children and teenagers. For many, the culmination of this process comes in high school—a time when it might have seemed like the *cool* or *popular* kids could do whatever they wanted, while the normal and less-popular kids experienced a much different reality.

The general assumption is that popular kids probably had better social skills and were often more humorous or entertaining than their less-popular classmates, but is that really all it takes to achieve high social status?

Popularity, whatever it is, is a quantity that people want no matter the circumstance.

Motivation and Popularity

Given the choice, it's a fair bet that just about everybody would prefer popularity and the accompanying social validation to the alternative. It simply feels good to be well-liked and respected by our peers. To achieve traditional popularity requires some amount of effort to socialize and connect with people, and that effort requires energy. Everybody has a limited supply of energy, and so being highly motivated to spend that energy socializing is a significant part of what it takes to be popular.

In reality, of course, not everybody wants to be popular to the same extent as everybody else. And as it turns out, there is a strong correlation between how rewarding popularity feels to people and how popular they actually are.

Dr. Dianna Martinez and her team of research colleagues at Columbia University found evidence that showed that there was a positive correlation between higher social status and social support and the density of dopamine type 2 (D2) and type 3 (D3) receptors in the striatum—a region of the brain that is largely responsible for our feelings of reward and motivation, something that dopamine plays a critical role in producing.

Normal and healthy volunteers were assessed to determine their social status and social support and were subsequently scanned using positron emission tomography, a technology that enables us to see D2 receptors in the brain.

The volunteers who had denser D2 receptors were the same ones who had the most social status, which suggests that popular individuals are more likely to experience life as rewarding and stimulating as a direct result of having more targets for dopamine to take effect within the striatum. They literally had different brain structures.

Dr. Martinez summed up the results by saying, "We showed that low levels of dopamine receptors were associated with low social status and that high levels of dopamine receptors were associated with higher social status. The same type of association was seen with the volunteer's reports of social support they experience from their friends, family, or significant other."

This contradicts our earlier theory that personality traits were the underlying cause behind popularity. It is in fact the type of brain structure and dopamine production you employ that might give rise to certain personality traits that result in popularity.

The editor of *Biological Psychiatry*, Dr. John Krystal, commented on the results of the study and said, "These data shed interesting light into the drive to achieve social status, a basic social process. It would make sense that people who had higher levels of D2 receptors, i.e., were more highly motivated and engaged by social situations, would be high achievers and would have higher levels of social support."

Popular people enjoyed people and social situations more, which will naturally make you more extroverted and charming.

At this point, you may be wondering what you can do to take advantage of this new information. Is there a way to safely and naturally increase the density of dopamine receptors in our brains?

Well, yes, kind of. There are chemicals called dopamine antagonists that are used to treat psychological conditions by artificially lowering dopamine, causing dopamine receptor density to increase in order to bring your brain back to an equilibrium state. However, these options come with loads of undesirable side effects and are not realistic for most.

Before you get discouraged, though, there are some realistic ways to increase your dopamine receptors—or rather, avoid desensitizing them—that don't come with the dangerous side effects. It basically involves doing fewer of the activities that artificially increase our dopamine levels—excessive Internet and TV use, coffee, recreational drugs, alcohol, watching pornography, or consuming a lot of sugar and processed food. Generally speaking, if you are addicted to something unhealthy, it's likely because that thing is giving you a hit of dopamine, which makes you feel good temporarily but has a long-term numbing effect on your motivation and reward behaviors by decreasing your sensitivity to dopamine.

In essence, starve yourself of dopamine until you spend time with people. Making conscious choices to do fewer of the things that give us those quick and easily repetitive dopamine hits will have a positive long-term impact on our feelings of motivation and reward in social situations, which in turn can help us to become more popular.

Social Sensitivity

In addition to being biologically predisposed to seek popularity due to greater dopamine receptor density, popular people have another interesting biological difference as compared to people with lower social status. The brains of popular people are more sensitive to social changes in their environment.

You may have wondered how the people you know with high social status achieved that level of popularity and influence. On a surface level, it probably seems that those people are simply friendly and fun to be around. While that is likely the case, research published in *Proceedings of the National Academy of Sciences* suggests that there is likely something much deeper going on that we aren't as aware of.

Scientists conducted brain-imaging studies that showed a common denominator between all of the popular participants: their brains are more sensitively attuned to the popularity of other people on a subconscious level. This means they are more empathetic and self-aware of relationships across social groups. This indicates that popular people are, at least in good part, popular because they *care* about being popular on a fundamental level.

The research was performed at Columbia University by Noam Zerubavel and a team of his colleagues. They recruited 26 student volunteers from two school clubs to participate and had each volunteer rate how much they liked every other individual in their club. The scores were summed for each participant and the final numbers were used to rank all of the members by likability or popularity.

The students then lay in brain scanners and were shown photos of the faces of their peers, in addition to an occasional "ghost face"—a morphed average of all of the other faces. As an experimental control, the students were told that their task was to instinctually press a key for each face that was presented indicating whether they thought it was a real person or a ghost face. The reality, of course, was that the researchers only wanted to see how their brain activity varied according to the popularity of the person they were currently presented with.

There were two main issues at hand that researchers wanted to work out. First, they wanted to see whether or not participants' brains responded differently according to the popularity of the person in the photos they were shown. After that, they wanted to analyze whether popular people's brains, in particular, responded differently to the exercise relative to those of their less-popular classmates.

The results were interesting on both fronts.

Independently of their own popularity levels, when participants were shown photos of more popular peers, their brains subsequently displayed more neural activity in the "social cognition system" involved in understanding how other people think and perceive us. This suggests that the more we care about a person's popularity, the more motivated we are to consider and analyze what they might be thinking.

It's hard to sugarcoat that evidence—people, on average, simply seem to devote more cognitive resources to you the more social status you have. This can certainly explain why being popular is desirable, but it can also be a curse to somebody who attains higher social status and isn't able to keep their ego in check when they inevitably get treated with greater regard.

When it came to the more popular participants, images of their neural responses showed that they had even greater sensitivity to social structure. All of the participants showed different activity levels based on the popularity of the person they were looking at, but those activity levels varied more widely in popular people than unpopular people. This lends a plausible explanation as to how they ascended to popularity in the first place—having a sharper awareness of the popularity of others enables them to selectively hang out more with the people who have high social status. The finding is also in line with prior psychological research that showed popular children tend to be more aware of who's popular and who isn't.

At a fundamental level, this provides a solid explanation for how social cliques form and why it can be so difficult for somebody new to integrate themselves into a different clique. Part of being popular is hanging out with other popular people, and the members of your public social circle likely play a significant role in how your own popularity is perceived by others. How to become accepted by them is another matter to be covered throughout this book, but understanding social status and what changes it is a key to popularity.

Dominance versus Prestige

Beyond differences in brain architecture, there are two predominant and more controllable approaches to achieve social status—*dominance* and *prestige*. A focus on either of these two factors, with moderation and good taste, can help you move up any social hierarchy.

Being dominant means being stronger, more intimidating, or more powerful than other people. Having prestige, on the other hand, means being more skilled, successful, and knowledgeable than the average person. At first glance, these are the traditional paths to being popular.

Especially when we are young, it can seem as if dominance is the best or even the only method of gaining the respect and admiration of our peers. Often, it's the schoolyard bullies who use intimidation, coercion, and fear-inducing tactics who appear to be the top dogs. Meanwhile, the students who put in the effort to get high grades in school are rarely socially rewarded for doing so at the time, at least in Western cultures. Those who get good grades do, however, have greater opportunities for further education and more impactful careers down the line so that they might be recognized and respected for their skills, success, and knowledge later in life.

Joseph Henrich and Gil White studied dominance and prestige within the context of sociology, sociolinguistics, ethnography, and ethnology. They found that the two paths to social status evolved separately and for different purposes.

A person's mental and physical dispositions will naturally determine which strategy, or hybrid of the two strategies, is most useful to employ in any given situation. Somebody who grows up in a less-progressive society or finds themselves in a highly adversarial environment, such as a prison, might find that the ability to intimidate others or enforce threats is the most effective way to reach the upper echelon of the social hierarchy. And of course, if they have a tendency to challenge and fight, or have natural physical strength, you can guess which path they will take. For those who find themselves in social environments that lack dominance hierarchies, having the mental skills necessary to acquire knowledge and create ideas that are valuable to society will make them more inclined to attain social status through prestige.

Now consider what routes you may be able to take to increase your own social status. It requires an honest assessment of your traits, strengths, and weaknesses so you can effectively use what you've got and minimize flaws. During this process, keep in mind that there are pitfalls to both options if they lack the proper subtlety.

For example, you may gain some authority over others if you become extremely dominant like the big bully from grade school, but is that really worth it if you sacrifice a good deal of likability in the process? People respond well to others who are confident and self-assured, but not when it's taken to the extremes of being cocky or self-absorbed.

Physicality may also play a major role in dominance, as somebody who is big in stature might have an easier time pulling it off than somebody who isn't particularly tall or strong. But how much of physical dominance is based on stature and how much is based on visible health and fitness? An obese person who is six feet tall and weighs 250 pounds is a lot less intimidating, on average, than somebody who is also six feet tall and 250 pounds but is a bodybuilder, for example.

What about the prestige route? Though perhaps a bit less obvious, there are still plenty of pitfalls with this strategy as well.

An intelligent and knowledgeable individual will be much less likely to attain social status through prestige if they are constantly reminding people of how smart and successful they are. It often requires a good deal of finesse to make people aware of your intellectual prowess without giving off the impression of being arrogant or judgmental. And being highly skilled, successful, and knowledgeable won't mean much socially if you don't have the communication skills to convey that in a way the average person can understand and appreciate.

The key here is to realize that it is possible to take shortcuts and achieve some success, but it's certainly not advisable. A person who needs to put others down in order to look dominant will eventually end up just looking insecure. A physical trainer without the knowledge or discipline to be healthy and fit personally will not be trusted by others who want to become healthy and fit themselves. Dominance and prestige are what people naturally look for, and you can increase your standing in both of those respects easily.

No matter how you choose to go about climbing up the social hierarchy, being genuine as well as conscious of how others perceive you throughout the process will certainly increase your odds for success. We're not all born with brains tailor-made for social success, but not all of us are born to be able to play basketball professionally. That doesn't mean we can't improve upon our natural traits and take a shortcut or two into what we know is instinctually valued.

Chapter 3. The Value of Shutting Up

We often think of people who are talkative and outgoing as some of the most skilled socializers there are, as they can prevent awkward silences and make others more comfortable by shouldering the brunt of the social burden in a given situation.

This chapter, however, is about the value of having a filter when you speak and understanding when it's time to simply shut up. At one time or another, everybody will eventually experience times when silence is appropriate, as well as times when an acquaintance, friend, or partner just needs somebody to listen to them talk for a little while.

There won't be any scientific studies in this chapter, because knowing when it's best to stay quite is mostly a matter of developing strong intuition, perception, and common sense. Having a big mouth can land you into some really big trouble, so it is greatly important to know what *not* to say and when *not* to make your presence known.

Pick Your Battles

One of the easiest mistakes for people to make socially is to get so attached to their ideas and thoughts that they are willing to harm their relationships for the sake of being "right." This is especially common in the case of interpersonal conflicts, when we are more emotionally sensitive and vulnerable and thus less likely to think clearly and rationally.

Have you ever said a lot of things that you thought were important in the heat of the moment, only to realize a few minutes or maybe days afterwards that it really didn't matter that much? Or worse, have you ever realized that you damaged a relationship with somebody you care about because you let your emotions carry you away?

Sometimes the best thing that we can do for ourselves is to relax a bit and to get in the habit of letting things slide instead of taking everything too seriously. We simply don't need to make every argument at every opportunity, and doing so is detrimental to our social success.

With a little introspection, you might also realize that you argue passionately over perceived transgressions—not because of the transgressions themselves—but because they hurt your sense of pride. Naturally, you're a lot more likely to say something regrettable when you're feeling insecure or threatened, as those fear-associated feelings lead to instinct overriding reason. By practicing mindfulness and self-awareness, however, you can cut off these harmful defense patterns and avoid saying things you'll regret later on.

You might be thinking that it's not always that straightforward to pick your battles, however.

You'd be right, sometimes the correct decision between being agreeable or being assertive isn't that obvious. You need to know when to shut up and when to stand your ground, and when that line is blurry, you'll need to rely on awareness and experience to determine a course of action. Asking yourself whether this will matter to you 30 days from now can be a really simple way to assess the importance of speaking up.

And for those times when it just isn't worth it, one of the best ways to avoid unnecessary conflict is by pretending not to hear what others have said. When you choose to be the bigger person and keep the peace instead of getting emotional, you show maturity and self-confidence that will improve your perception among other socially skilled people.

Imagine that you overhear a colleague at work saying that they are better at the job than you.

Either they have a good point and you should focus on improving your work, or they are insecure about their own job and trying to feel better by putting you down, in which case confronting them is probably going to go poorly. Your colleagues likely don't appreciate being brought into other people's drama, so being defensive and talking to them isn't expected to win you any likeability points there, either. But not saying anything, and just doing well at your job? That makes the bad-mouther look illegitimate and wins you respect among your peers because you showed maturity and professionalism.

You'll save yourself a lot trouble in life if you just shut up and accept that you won't always get things your way. But don't worry, this will help you in the long run. Impressions are often formed by how people see you respond to hardship.

Listen More and Brag Less

All of us are self-interested to an extent, some much more so than others. Keeping this in mind when we socialize can make a world of difference in how likeable we are and how much people want to foster relationships with us.

The first way to utilize an awareness of this human trait is to appease other people's desire to talk about themselves by listening to them and showing interest in what they are talking about. This makes the conversation enjoyable for the person you are talking to, and also gives them social validation, which makes them feel good about sharing their thoughts with you. That's exactly what you want! Give them the spotlight and provide encouragement as they open up so that they can gain confidence in themselves and trust in you.

The people whom you like best and choose to spend time with most often are very likely the people who make you feel the best in their company. Feeling comfortable and accepted allows us to express ourselves openly, which naturally leaves a better impression than feeling awkward, judged, or bored. You can use this to your advantage by being genuinely curious about people you meet or already know, and seeing what you can learn from listening to what they have to say.

Suppose that you're making small talk with a new acquaintance, and they start venting about their work. Sounds like it will be an unpleasant interaction, right? Now you can half-listen to them for the sake of politeness and then interrupt as quickly as possible, or you can take a sincere interest in them and try to make a connection. You might try to learn why they are unhappy with their work, and what they would rather be doing instead. By being engaged, you at least give yourself the chance to steer the conversation from a negative subject to a passion or an interest they have, which will make them feel better and will hopefully be more enjoyable for you, too.

On the other side of the coin, we have the braggers—the people who just won't shut up about their accomplishments and how amazing they are. You want to do everything you can to not be one of these people, because just about everybody finds excessive bravado annoying.

Something that people who brag a lot often don't realize is that it leaves others with an impression that you are overcompensating and that you lack vulnerability—making it more difficult to connect with you. Additionally, boasting will give the appearance that you are trying to be someone you are not—an unconfident look that a lot of people will see straight through. Braggers also tend to be sensitive to criticism and overly defensive, which only adds to the unpleasantness of their company.

Perhaps the most annoying thing that a bragger will do is constantly try to one-up other people. Let's say somebody is really excited about losing 15 pounds and getting into better shape, and instead of congratulating or encouraging them, you start talking about your own fitness accomplishments and steal all of the thunder. Frankly, nobody cares about how fit you are, and this doesn't make you look cool at all. It just makes everybody think you're self-centered and rude, and it might be dejecting to the person who was excited about their weight loss.

As a general rule, you'll be perceived more positively by others when you make the effort to listen more often than you talk and to show real interest in what other people have to say. A little pat on your own back every now and again doesn't hurt, but if you are constantly talking yourself up, it's going to be counterproductive for achieving more social success.

So remember to just shut up about yourself because, even though you might see yourself as the center of the universe, other people don't.

Stop With "Brutal" Honesty and Stop Giving Unsolicited Advice

How many times have you heard somebody excuse rude and hurtful comments by claiming that they are simply calling it how they see it, or being brutally honest? Going even further, it's often just an excuse to insult someone or be an overall ass*ole. Chances are you've come across a few people who communicate this way, and it's also probable that they weren't the most likable people you've ever encountered.

Brutal honesty most often means criticizing others without any tact or sense of compassion. Supposedly, those blunt comments and criticisms are meant to be beneficial to whomever they are directed at, and they are only hurtful if taken personally or defensively.

The thing about brutal honesty, though, is that nobody actually prefers it, and in most cases, it just comes across as deliberately mean. The vast majority of the time, negativity just isn't necessary because it's possible to accomplish your goal by providing feedback or criticism in a mature and considerate way. Complaining and nitpicking about things that aren't important just makes you come across as judgmental and abrasive—making others feel small so that you can feel big.

Honesty itself is very useful, and having the tact to be honest in a way that doesn't put people down is an invaluable life skill to have. But far too many people think that honesty is socially acceptable in any form. The simple truth of the matter is that if you want to always say how you feel without any kind of a filter, people just won't like you. Unless, of course, you are the first brutally honest person ever to think and feel positive things all the time.

There's a particular type of brutal honesty, tough love, that's commonly used by parents to teach their young children important lessons. But tough love is not for everyone or every situation, and is probably even counterproductive for raising children in a lot of scenarios, as the lesson they learn may come with an unhealthy hit to their self-esteem.

Anytime that you feel the need to criticize somebody, ask if that criticism can actually help them. If not, keep it to yourself. If so, frame it in a tactful way that doesn't come off as a personal attack.

For example, say you've got a friend who dresses really poorly and it adversely affects their attractiveness to others. If that's something your friend cares about and would want to know, then a productive way to help your friend is to suggest something that you think would look good on them, and then compliment them when they do dress well in order to give positive reinforcement. Except in serious cases, positive reinforcement can work a whole lot better than criticism—especially criticism that's framed as honesty, but lacking any practical advice.

But now let's imagine that your friend has never given any indication that they want to improve their attractiveness or that they care about their wardrobe. Now anything you say in the form of advice is unsolicited, which just makes you annoying.

As a general rule, giving unsolicited advice isn't going to be received well, no matter how good your intentions are. When people vent or rant to you about some problems in their lives, the socially intelligent response is to let them fulfill their purpose for speaking without interrupting them to interject your own solution. Talking about problems serves as emotional catharsis—meaning that it's often a solution all of its own, and you can be a part of that solution just by listening.

Finally, one of the most socially counterproductive things you can do is to make pedantic corrections of people. Anything that indirectly implies that you are above others will make you less likeable, plain and simple. You may think that people want or should want to be corrected when they error, but when those errors are unimportant and don't hurt anybody, it's not your responsibility or social prerogative to point them out.

So do yourself and everybody else a favor— shut up and stop interjecting your opinions and advice when nobody asks or cares to hear them.

The common theme from each of these social mistakes that people make is that they can be avoided just by shutting up more often. You may only exhibit one or two of these behaviors personally, or even none of them if you are already highly skilled socially. It's also possible that, through introspection, you could realize you are guilty of almost all of them from time to time.

It's good to analyze when you've made these mistakes in the past, as it can show the areas that you should personally focus on building more awareness in the future. That being said, there's no use in beating yourself up over those mistakes, because we all do these things to some degree. Not knowing when to shut up doesn't automatically make you unlikable; it simply inhibits you from reaching your full social potential.

If you build your awareness about when it's appropriate to talk and when it's better to listen or be silent, you'll improve the depth of your relationships and be more enjoyable company for the people in your life. In the famous words of the 19th century actor Will Rogers, "Never miss a good chance to shut up."

Chapter 4. Just Be Positive? Really?

No doubt you've heard about the power of positivity countless times throughout your life. Motivational speakers, successful entrepreneurs, and world-class athletes consistently seem to give some variation of that simple piece of advice—just be positive and everything you are seeking will magically come your way.

But is that just a tired cliché, or is there some scientific evidence to support positivity as an effective means of being socially successful and well-regarded by others? After all, you would think that people wouldn't keep repeating it if they didn't feel like it contributed to their success a bit.

As it turns out, there is some scientific evidence, but it might not be for the reasons that you would expect. This chapter will dive into research that shows the surprising value of being happy and positive for your social success and likability. It's good to maintain a healthy level of skepticism around such blanket statements of success formulae, but in this case the research is telling.

Interconnectedness

All of us on this planet are connected in such a way that our emotions can spread to one another and be felt incredibly easily. And this isn't just limited to face-to-face interactions, but actually includes influencing and being influenced by people we don't even know exist.

At first, it can be a bit hard to believe that this is the case. It sounds more reasonable to say that we can impact the people whom we interact with closely, but it's a far bigger step to say that our personal state of being at any given time actually affects just about everything around us. But think about how you feel about seeing particularly happy or sad news on the television, or the last movie you cried at. You'll realize how we can affect each other's psyches more than you thought possible.

A study conducted at Harvard University showed that our happiness seems to radiate from us like an energy field—capable of reaching and impacting the people around us. Between 1983 and 2003, the team of Harvard researchers followed 4,739 volunteers around and measured the effects that peoples' happiness could have on their families, friends, neighbors, and social networks. The study's published results including some truly incredible findings:

- Your chances of happiness increase by 42% when a friend who lives within half a mile of you gets happy.

- Your chances of happiness increase by "only" 25% if that happy friend lives a mile away from you.
- Siblings who live close to a happy sibling increase their chances of happiness by 14%.
- Next-door neighbors of a happy person have a 35% higher likelihood of happiness.

The fact that happiness is spreadable was even more apparent when the researchers graphed the social networks that they were studying according to each participant's physical location. Every individual in the network was represented by a dot that was colored on a spectrum according to that person's happiness, with blue being the unhappy end of the spectrum and yellow being the happy end. Rather than a seemingly random distribution of colors like you might expect, similar colors tended to form clusters with each other, indicating that our emotional states are not at all independent of our physical surroundings.

The results were explained by one of the authors of the study, Dr. Christakis, who said,

"You would think that your emotional state would depend on your own choices and actions and experience, but it also depends on the choices and actions and experiences of other people, including people to whom you are not directly connected. Happiness is contagious." James H. Fowler, his coauthor, added to this by saying, *"We need to think of happiness as a collective phenomenon. If I come home in a bad mood, I may be missing an opportunity to make not just my wife and son happy, but their friends."*

What can you do with this knowledge about the amazing contagiousness of positivity? The answer to that can be broken into to two main pieces.

The first is determining, to whatever extent possible, whom we spend the majority of our time around and how that impacts our emotional state. If you are surrounded by happy people, the evidence suggests that you will be much more likely to be happy yourself. And if being close to one happy friend can make you 42% more likely to be happy yourself, just imagine what two, five, ten, or fifty happy friends could do for you. At the same time, think about the effects of having those same numbers of friends in your life if they are often grumpy, annoyed, unhappy, or otherwise psychologically negative influences.

It's impossible to control your environment completely, but choosing friends wisely certainly seems to be one of the healthiest decisions we can make for our own well-being.

The second thing that you can think about and act upon when it comes to contagious positivity is being a hub for positivity personally. Indeed, this is where all the cliché advice leads to—just be positive! But as mentioned, it's not necessarily for the reasons typically espoused. In reality, if you are happy yourself, you'll be able to indirectly spread that to everybody around you. Being able to make other people feel good in your presence is about as valuable a social skill as there is because they'll simply want you around more, miss you when you're not, and desire your presence.

Not only that, but you can try to impact another person's happiness directly by being nice or complimentary to them, or just having a positive mindset when you interact with them. The more happiness you spread, the more it can come back around to you.

If you aren't particularly witty, entertaining, or outgoing, simply cultivating a positive attitude can be the most worthwhile first step in gaining social status.

The Theory of Social and Emotional Contagion

The theory of social and emotional contagion essentially describes how emotions can be shared from one person to another more easily than you would think, with happiness and positivity being only one facet of that.

The idea that there is interpersonal influence, known as "emotional contagion," has been recognized by psychologists for over half a century—beginning with Schachter in 1959, but also including works by Cacioppo and Petty in 1987 as well as by Levy and Nail in 1993, to name a few.

One of the most important and widely cited studies on this phenomenon was conducted by Sigal G. Barsade at Yale University in 2002. Barsade's study was titled "The Ripple Effect: Emotional Contagion and Its Influence on Group Behavior."

The study's participants, business school students, were broken up into small groups for a simulated management exercise. Each student was asked to role-play a department head who would advocate for their employee to get as large a merit-based bonus as possible. At the same time, all the students were expected to work together in a committee that determined how best to allocate a limited pot of funds in a way that would provide the most overall benefit to the company.

Unbeknownst to the study participants, there was also an actor inserted into each group who was trained to convey one of four different mood conditions: cheerful enthusiasm, serene warmth, hostile irritability, and depressed sluggishness.

So how much do you think the emotional state portrayed by that single actor in each group could impact all of the unaware students during the negotiation?

The results revealed a significant effect of emotional contagion. The actors that conveyed cheerful enthusiasm or serene warmth spread those feelings to the other members of their groups, who then displayed greater cooperation and less interpersonal conflict with each other. In addition, these groups actually made decisions that allocated the bonus funds more equitably than the other groups, and they reported having more positive feelings about their individual performances than their counterparts in the groups that had actors conveying negative emotions.

Interestingly, when the students were asked what had caused them to allocate the funds the way they had, as well as why their group had performed the way it did, they most commonly attributed it to their personal negotiating acumen, or the qualities of the "candidates" on whose behalf they were negotiating. They didn't even suspect that their behavior and decisions, or those of their group, had been steered by the emotional state of an actor.

You can probably see how significant a role this emotional contagion effect can have on your popularity. If your likability has a lot to do with how people feel in your presence, and the actual emotional nature of your presence can impact how people feel, then you have a direct method to become more likable.

By being consciously positive and putting on a happy face more often than not, you can impart that positivity onto your peers and use your social influence to create more cooperative and friendly environments around you. At the same time, your negative emotional states are just as powerful in the opposite way. When you're feeling irritable, sluggish, or sad, you should still try to put on a happy face while socializing, lest you infect your friends or colleagues with your negative emotions. Misery doesn't just love company; it also creates it.

If you've ever been to a sporting event where you were cheering for the "away" team, you've had a chance to experience the power of the emotional contagion phenomenon at scale.

When you watch a game on the TV, either alone or with a small group, your emotional state is mostly going to be determined by the performance of the team you want to win. But when you are in a stadium or arena and surrounded by thousands of fans who are full of energy and rooting for the opposite side, it can feel like your team's performance doesn't affect you to nearly the same degree as it normally would.

When things go poorly for your team but the home crowd is pumped up with positive energy as a result, it's almost difficult to not be a part of that positive energy, too. And when your team does well, but that makes everybody around you feel negative, you probably won't enjoy your team's success as much as you might if you were watching at home. Of course, there are instances of extreme fanaticism or genuine animosity between fans that might mitigate these effects, but in most cases, they will hold true.

There is just no getting around the fact that our emotions will impact others and that we will likewise be impacted by theirs. Achieving social success, therefore, starts with being a positive influence on others and removing or diminishing the negative influences on ourselves.

The Healthy Effects of Positivity

Positivity might still seem like a somewhat abstract thing to you, not something that can be easily controlled or imitated. In reality, however, the "fake it until you make it" philosophy that has been shown to be effective for gaining confidence can actually work for positivity, too, and emotional contagion is a big part of that. When you make a real effort to present yourself as positive through facial expressions, body language, and communication, your brain won't know the difference. Moreover, the people around you can be influenced by your positive state—genuine or not—and they, in turn, can radiate that positivity back to you and make a real impact on your mood.

Feeling positive means not being stressed or anxious, and in turn not activating the subsequent fight or flight reaction that is obviously detrimental to us in social situations. When you are stuck in a negative mindset, your brain can't clearly see all of the options and choices around you and you enter into survival mode, an unhealthy place to be when your life isn't actually on the line. Imagine creating that effect in others.

Showing and spreading positive emotions like joy, contentment, and love will allow you to see more possibilities in your life. Researchers in behavioral psychology have continued to find evidence suggesting that positive thinking opens up your mind to more options and creates real value for your health and well-being.

What's really important to remember from all of this is that everybody is interconnected socially, and you are emitting emotional signals constantly for other people to pick up—for better or worse. If social success is what you're after, being aware of your impact on others and making it a positive one is an excellent place to start.

Positivity is a choice, but to make positivity a consistent part of who you are will take practice and discipline as you build healthier habits. There are countless ways that people recommend to help you become more positive, and some may be more helpful for you than others. A few of the ones that generally make a big difference for people are expressing more gratitude, removing negative words like "can't" from your vocabulary, and being more compassionate and forgiving of yourself, just to name a few. Whatever happens in your life, just remember that you always have the choice to take a positive outlook.

Chapter 5. Perception Part One

As soon as you see somebody whom you are going to interact with, you probably begin sizing them up subconsciously. Do they look friendly or standoffish, anxious or calm, energetic or sluggish, and so on?

The way that you perceive others, both in those initial encounters and subsequently, can play a very significant role in your social success and personal likeability. Your perception of the people you interact with impacts what you think of them, how you approach them, how you feel about them, and the impressions that you give them of you.

The power of the first impression is sometimes shocking in how it can persist in subconscious and sneaky ways.

Only this time, it's about the impressions you make about other people that are potentially harmful to you. Being aware of the role of perception during interactions, therefore, is a valuable skill to find social success.

The Gain-Loss Principle

Whenever you are reading peoples' body language and facial expressions before and during interactions with them, it's likely that they are doing the same thing with you. The more the other person seems to like you, the more you will probably accept and like them.

This dynamic is at the center of what's known as the *gain-loss principle*, which states that as one person's opinion of somebody else becomes increasingly favorable, the other person is more likely to develop a more favorable opinion of them in return.

The most dramatic effects of the gain-loss principle can be seen when people begin with an initially unfavorable opinion of someone else, and then at some point transition to a more favorable opinion of them for whatever reason. If this were to happen to somebody's perception of you, it would—more likely than not—result in a similarly positive change in how much you like the other person as well.

Psychologists Elliot Aronson and Darwyn Linder hypothesized that this principle of interpersonal attraction existed, and so they conducted an experiment in 1965 to test it. The study involved staging meetings between volunteer participants and a "confederate"— the term used to identify an actor who is often used in social science research as a means of purposefully influencing the subjects in order to set the stage or to elicit some kind of reaction.

In this case, the confederates were used to manipulate subjects in order to test how much our opinions of others depend upon their opinions of us. The researchers did this by asking the confederates for their opinions of the study participants before and after the confederates had interviewed them, and they did so intentionally within earshot of the participants so that they could overhear.

Afterwards, the participants were asked to fill out a form that included several questions related to their opinions of the confederate whom they had met and overheard talking about them. The results showed that the study subjects tended to like the confederate the most when the confederate had started with a low opinion of them but later reported a better opinion. In the reverse situation, in which the confederate started with a high opinion and then switched to a lower one, the subjects reported that they liked the confederate the least. In both scenarios when the confederate's opinion didn't change, the participants had milder opinions of them.

Michael Palmer, Ph.D., states that if a person increases their positive feelings for you, then you are likely to do the same for them, plain and simple. We can take advantage of this phenomenon by exhibiting pleasant behavior toward the people we interact with through a positive presence and increased affections when it's appropriate. And if there are people for whom you start out with a negative opinion, switching to liking them will have an even greater effect.

An important thing to notice from the study is that the participants learned the confederate's opinion of them subtly, not through direct compliments or affection. You can take advantage of the same subtlety by making sure that your gossip about friends and acquaintances is positive. If you are always talking people up when they aren't around, that information can get back to them and automatically give them a more favorable view of you.

When you do want to be more direct, you can take advantage of the gain-loss principle in how you compliment others. For example, you might say, "When I first met you I thought [insert negative/neutral personality trait], but now that I've gotten to know you, I can see that you're actually [insert positive personality trait]." When you compliment a friend in this way, you make them feel that they've won you over, which will make them like you more in return.

Another interesting facet of the gain-loss principle comes from a 1965 study conducted at the University of Minnesota, which suggested that complimenting or otherwise commenting positively has a greater impact on the recipient if you only do it occasionally.

The team of research psychologists broke the participants—80 female college students—into pairs in order to perform a task, and then, as with the Aronson and Linder experiment, allowed the students to "overhear" their partners talking about them. However, the researchers had instructed half of the partners on what to say beforehand in order to observe the results. Some students said negative or positive comments both before and after, while others switched from positive to negative and vice versa.

The results indicated that the partners whose comments started negative and then became positive were the most liked, more so than those that were always positive. As was the case in the first study, the participants felt the most positively about the people whom they had won over.

So what else can we learn from this study? If you want people to like you, it's still good to be complimentary sometimes, but be careful not to overdo it. Just make it known that you like them and see them as a friend or ally. Don't hold them at arm's length or appear guarded, because they will reciprocate. However, if you are excessively positive or complimentary to the point that you come across as ingenuine or clingy, you likely won't achieve the social success you're looking for.

An occasional thoughtful compliment can make them feel a lot better than consistent shallow compliments—especially if you can contrast it with how you felt negatively about them before, and their actions were so great that you had no choice but to change your mind.

Pygmalion Effect

Acting the part of a good friend is helpful, but just as helpful is not judging others and putting a set of expectations on them—which makes them become who we think they are.

This is known as the Pygmalion Effect, named for the mythical Greek figure who fell in love with his own sculpture. It states that if you have an image of that person's behavior and personality, that's exactly who they'll become.

The implication is that however you view someone, you will treat them in a way that brings that behavior out of them. If you think someone is incredibly annoying, you will be standoffish toward them and generally act in a manner that is actually annoying in and of itself, motivating them to behave annoyingly. If you think well of someone, you will act toward them in a manner that encourages them to be better and you will give them more chances; if you think poorly of someone, you will act toward them in a manner that will make them do worse and you won't give them the benefit of the doubt.

The Pygmalion Effect was discovered in 1979 in a study conducted on students and teacher by Robert Feldman. Students were given IQ tests, and the teachers were not told the results. However, the teachers were told that specific students comprising 20% of the class were gifted and had extremely high IQs. These students were randomly selected.

At the end of the school year, the students took another IQ test, and the 20% who were randomly selected had the largest gain in IQ— the ones the teachers thought were the smartest. What did this mean? The teachers subconsciously or consciously treated them differently and gave them preferential treatment because they had a good impression of them and their intellect. The students became who the teachers thought they were. Thus, a key to likability is to have positive perceptions of people so that they can become who we think they are.

Never underestimate the power of your own expectations. You create the world you reside in through your expectations. If you were told someone was charming and fascinating, you would dig deeper into their background and discover what might be interesting about them. Conversely, if you were told that same person was a boring dud, you may not even bother engaging them. Our assumptions and expectations dictate our actions and create self-fulfilling prophecies.

In another example with children, suppose one parent decided her kids were smart, while one parent decided her kids weren't the sharpest tools in the shed. The first parent would help her child with homework, get them a tutor, and make sure they were fulfilling their potential for intelligence. The second parent would ignore her child's homework and tell them to apply themselves in other ways outside the classroom. There would be a huge disparity in attention and emphasis on studying, and thus the kids would turn out to fulfill their parents' expectations. They receive positive or negative feedback and the cycle grows.

We like to imagine that we are treating everyone equally, but that is essentially impossible if we think poorly of them. How can understanding the Pygmalion Effect help your likability?

Assume the best of the people you're speaking with and you will start treating them in a way that makes them like you more. Recall that people become who we expect them to be, so if we expect them to be charming and kind, we will bring that out of them. Above all else, you're going to be sending 100% positive and friendly signals to everyone—people tend to respond favorably to these. When people are kind to us, we tend to be kind to them in return, and the Pygmalion Effect is broken.

Cognitive and Processing Fluency

Many people have an idea that appearing complex and mysterious to others will intrigue them, and that this is a viable method of creating social success. It may actually work here and there, but this strategy will be mostly counterproductive.

That's because of what's known as *cognitive and processing fluency*—the ease with which information can be processed by our brains. The fundamental implication of cognitive and processing fluency is that we like things that are simple and quickly understood. The term actually comes from marketing, where it is applied in many areas including core components of a business's identity such as brand naming and logo design. What is easily understood tends to stick in our brains longer and be subconsciously more likable.

It makes a lot of sense in the marketing world, which is filled with slogans like "Just do it," and applying processing fluency to a social context simply suggests that it's in our best interest to appear familiar and similar to others so that they can understand us instantly and thus like us more.

We are naturally more receptive to information that appears simple, and we are put off by things that appear overly complex. For personal interactions, anything that affects processing fluency can—and does—have an impact on how others will perceive you. As a result, there are many seemingly insignificant aspects of how we present ourselves that end up making a real difference in our social success.

One example of how impactful processing fluency can be comes from a study conducted in 2008 at the University of Michigan. Two researchers, Hyunjin Song and Norbert Schwarz, studied the influence of typography on our experience of fluency and disfluency.

Song and Schwarz gave study participants instructions for anything from exercise regimes to cooking recipes, and they varied the fonts from basic and clear to more fancy and complex styles. They found that for the exact same set of instructions, font type directly affected how difficult the task seemed to the readers. The less simple and easy to read the font was, the greater the tendency to rate the task outlined in the instructions as more complicated. In other words, people were correlating the difficulty of reading the instructions with the difficulty of performing the task itself.

We can conclude, therefore, that the ease with which we can read instructions translates immediately onto our perception of how easy the task itself will be.

What does this mean? When we can't quickly and easily understand something or someone, we think of it as difficult and like it less. On the other hand, things that are easy to process and understand immediately are naturally more likable. We simply like things that are easy for us.

In terms of social success, then, your goal should be to appear simple (read: not complex or mysterious) so that others can understand who you are immediately and without much effort. But how can you actually use the ideas of cognitive fluency to make yourself quickly and easily understood?

It starts with that all-important first impression.

Whenever you are introducing yourself to somebody new, explain yourself in a simple and easy-to-understand way. Be conscious to speak loudly and clearly so that others don't have to struggle to listen to you. Appear to be honest to avoid making others spend effort analyzing your motives and whether or not you are trustworthy. And most of all, appear straightforward and direct—save your complex thoughts and nuanced beliefs for future interactions, and focus instead on presenting yourself to be a simple person with clear motivations.

If you think that it's not so easy to appear simple, there's something helpful you can do. Start by developing some sort of narrative for yourself, as if you are a character from a story or film. Do you have any core philosophies that guide your actions through life? Your present personality is a result of all of your past experiences—it's difficult to appear simple and to act consistently without a solid understanding of what you believe and why.

All of the great fictional characters have actions that make you think, "Oh, that makes sense," because of their background and story. James Bond doesn't ever get flustered, so eventually, he will find a way out of even the most perilous circumstances—usually with just seconds to spare. Harry Potter represents courage and love, so in the big moments of the series, he always acts out of those two dispositions. Both Harry Potter and James Bond, as well as all of the other great characters of our time, are inherently simple to understand. They are a certain way because of the things that happened to them in the past, just like us.

When you have a narrative and you apply it consistently, your statements and behaviors will appear to all make sense and form an easily understood picture of yourself. That makes it simpler and more efficient for people to process information about you, which in turn makes you more likable than you would otherwise be as a complex and inconsistent person.

Being likable is ultimately a very crucial part of achieving genuine social success in our modern society. And at the core of likeability is the question of how you perceive others and how they perceive you in return.

The gain-loss principle and its supporting evidence help us to understand that when we like others, they're significantly more likely to like us back, plain and simple. The Pygmalion Effect piggybacks on this by making the equation depend in part on allowing people to be charming to you.

And when it comes to those ultra-important first impressions, don't try to seem complex, deep, aloof, or mysterious. For every person whose attention you grab, you'll just confuse and deter the vast majority of the others.

Instead, give yourself a narrative and act accordingly, presenting yourself in a way that makes it easy for others to understand you.

Chapter 6. Perception Part Two

It is difficult to overstate how important a role perception plays in our social success, and that's why there are two chapters devoted to it in this book. We learned in the first chapter that we have a tendency to preemptively judge people based on little to no information, and the basis of this judgment can have negative effects on socializing.

This second chapter will talk about some of the science behind the influence that your behavior toward other people has on how they act toward you. It's likely that you've observed this phenomenon a multitude of times in your own social experiences—the real question is whether or not you've figured out how to best utilize this knowledge to increase your social success.

Additionally, we will examine the nature of our responses to positive and negative feedback, and why sometimes the latter can actually make us feel better.

Reciprocity and Likeability

One of the more obvious behavioral tendencies we have as humans is what's known as reciprocity of liking—a phenomenon in which choosing to like somebody first makes it much more probable that they'll like you back.

The immediate application of this is simple— when you meet somebody new, make it known that you like them and you'll increase the odds of building a positive relationship with them.

Imagine for a moment that you've just met somebody completely new, had a brief conversation with them, and then parted ways. At this point, it's likely that neither of you has any strong feelings or impressions of the other. Now let's say that the next day, you're talking with a mutual friend or acquaintance who says, "Oh, that person you met yesterday was really impressed with you." With that small piece of information, your perception of that person is likely to change in a radical way. You might even be ready to call them a friend.

But if it was always that easy, why doesn't everybody just make it really obvious that they like people whom they want to form relationships with so that they can be socially successful? Before getting to that question, let's dive into a few of the studies so that we better understand when reciprocity of liking is applicable.

Reciprocal liking has been proven to be a powerful social tool in one clever study after the other. In the 1960s, Elliot Aronson and Phillip Worchel conducted a study at the

University of Texas that used confederate actors to test out reciprocal liking in a subtle way. Volunteers were broken into pairs and simply told to have a conversation with each other, after which they privately wrote brief statements about their reactions to the experiment as well as rating how much they liked their partners.

Unbeknownst to the volunteers, however, one of the two participants in each conversation was a confederate—a trained actor who was actually working with the researchers. For a random half of the conversations, the confederate would write a statement that said, "I enjoyed working with [my partner]; [he/she] seems like a really profound and interesting person." For the remaining half of conversations, they would write, "I did not enjoy working with [my partner] in the experiment; [he/she] seems like a really shallow and uninteresting person." After the confederates wrote the statements, the researchers allowed participants to read what their partners had written about them.

The results were unquestionably clear, and they've been replicated in countless studies since. The participants who read that their partners had liked them reported also liking their partners drastically more often than when they had read that their partners didn't like them.

What does this mean for us? And back to our earlier question—if this is easily observed, why don't people take better advantage of it?

The biggest conclusion that we can draw is that being the first to show your affection by outright saying to people that you like them will create a self-reinforcing cycle that will make people think more highly of you or like you more in return. Doing so, however, makes us vulnerable to rejection, which is the primary reason that reciprocity of liking isn't used as extensively as you might expect. Irrational as it may be, people don't like risking personal rejection under almost any circumstances, even when the odds of success far outweigh the odds of failure. Even if you say you like someone, they might not say it back.

Another possible reason for people not taking advantage of reciprocal liking more often is that it might come across as an ingenuine and therefore obvious tactic. In the case of our first example from this chapter, if your interaction is not only brief but also awkward, boring, or forgettable, when you hear that the person was impressed by you, it's possible that you'll simply be left wondering why. You may even think the other person is weird or faking being nice, two things that wouldn't lead to reciprocated liking.

If your compliment doesn't match up in some way with how the other person perceived the interaction, it's less likely to go over as well as you'd hope. Therefore, the most effective application of reciprocity of liking is quite often a subtle and authentic one. Don't compliment or express affection to others just for the sake of getting them to like you; find something real about them that you appreciate and focus on that.

If the majority of people bother, annoy, or bore you, then simply acting like you like them probably won't make a considerable difference. For many, being more likable to a greater number of people may actually entail taking a more positive view of people first.

If you're willing to be vulnerable and able to be authentic, you'll likely find that reciprocity of liking is a viable means of achieving new heights of social success.

Self-Verification Theory

What kind of roles do self-esteem and our general views about ourselves play in social likability as it relates to perception? Bill Swan, a psychologist from the University of Texas at Austin, published what's known as the self-verification theory in 1981 as an answer to that question.

The theory states that humans all desire to confirm our self-views and are naturally inclined to like people who help us do so, regardless of whether our views are positive or negative. Moreover, this desire to verify what we believe about ourselves is so powerful that it can actually override the desire for social approval and praise. We like to hear from others about how good of a skier we are, even if we aren't, because it verifies a belief of ours.

For people with high self-esteem and generally positive self-views, the theory makes intuitive sense. It's not surprising that people who believe that they are lovable, competent, and worthy would also desire for others to see them in a similarly positive way.

The theory becomes much more interesting, though, in the case of individuals with negative self-views, low self-esteem, or depressive symptoms. These people don't view themselves as particularly likable, lovable, competent, or worthy, so you might intuitively think that they would be highly motivated to seek out positive feedback in order to boost their self-image. But in fact, self-verification theory actually argues the opposite. Instead of compliments that make them feel better, these individuals prefer for others to see them in an equally unfavorable way as they see themselves.

We just want other people's views of us to be aligned with our own, regardless of the circumstances of our self-views. Even when our self-views are negative and therefore conflicting with our desire to maintain a positive image of ourselves, self-verification overrides that desire and is the stronger factor at play in how we feel about what others say about us.

Psychologists Paul White and Stephen Harkins discovered an indirect application of self-verification theory during a study that they conducted in 1994. The results of the study showed that white people cared more about messages given by black people than they did about those given by other white people, presumably because the white people wanted to confirm that they were not racist.

In this case, and perhaps others, the highest-valued views in our minds are those that allow us the greatest amount of self-verification. If you're somebody who's known as intelligent, or funny, or entertaining, complimenting other people on those same positive personality traits that you have can make them all the more impactful. You might feel more accomplished if you can make a comedian laugh as opposed to anybody else, and you may even like the comedian more because of it. Know what someone prides themselves on and let them know you appreciate that about them. Likewise, agree with them on their self-assessments and make it clear that you agree and speak that same language.

At this point, you might be wondering *why* the self-verification theory is true. What is it about verifying our self-views that we like so much that it's better than having other people view us as positively as possible?

The theory suggests that our reason for preferring self-verification comes down to control. We live in a chaotic world, and getting consistency between our opinions of ourselves and the feedback we receive from others engenders some sense of control in our lives. We can anticipate how others will treat us, think of us, and behave around us. Having a good idea of what to expect, even when it's negative, means that we aren't surprised in social situations, and thus we feel that we are in control. Moreover, when others verify our self-views, it gives us the impression that we know ourselves well, which also makes us feel better.

So if self-verification is all about control, what happens when we can't control the kinds of feedback we receive?

A study by Vicki Ritts and James Stein in 1995 found that people were less open and connected with their spouse if said spouse viewed them much differently than they viewed themselves—both when it was more positive and less so. Other studies, including one by Elizabeth Pinel and William Swann in 1996, have discovered that individuals are likely to experience anxiety if they are confronted by feedback that strongly contradicts their self-image. This is referred to as disintegration anxiety, and it can be characterized by a feeling that something is terribly wrong.

The desire for self-verification is a real and important factor in how everybody perceives each other in social situations. The question, then, is what you can do with this knowledge to achieve more social success.

First and foremost, pay attention to how people are trying to show themselves and then help them to verify that self-image. For example, if you have a friend who often wears unorthodox and extremely colorful outfits, you could tell that friend that you see them as a unique and expressive person. Simply make it known that you see the image that they are trying to cultivate.

Furthermore, always agree with people on their traits—strengths as well as weaknesses. Even when they have character traits that are rather obvious, you can say things like "I bet you like/want..." for whatever those traits may be and that will likely make them see you more favorably. If you want to boost somebody's self-image, don't just give them an ingenuine compliment; they likely won't believe and they'll think less of you for it. So try using a different approach—supposing your spouse is lacking confidence, you could say, "I think that you are low on confidence, but you shouldn't be because you are [genuine compliments about positive personality traits]." This type of confidence will go over much more smoothly because it is authentic and verifies your spouse's self-views, while also being positive.

When it comes to yourself, notice how you respond to various types of feedback as it relates to your self-views. If greater self-awareness and an accurate self-image are important to you, then recognizing that natural tendency to feel anxious and reject anything that contradicts your existing views of yourself may help you learn something new.

In-Group versus Out-Group Dynamics

Sometimes you meet people and you instantly hit it off. There's no explanation why, but it just seems that you have so much in common and every new thing they say seems to be exactly what you're thinking. From a simple comment about going to the same high school, to the fact that you both support the same basketball team, everything just seems to be working in your favor.

In these instances, you can't help but feel that your similarities make you somehow part of a group that others don't have access to. After all, you share so many interests and you're finding it impossible to disagree on anything. It's a small bond that you form in only a few moments, but from just a simple exchange, you will instantly find yourself favoring that person.

The study of in-groups versus out-groups reveals a lot about our identity and social psychology. We have a tendency to instantly like those we deem to be part of the same group that we ourselves are in. But why is this?

How can we feel such a close and exciting connection even without knowing someone very well?

In a famous study by Tajfel, Billig, Bundy, and Flament, in 1971, researchers studied how perceptions changed when you believed you were in a certain group. The study had a group of high school students come to a laboratory and look at a range of artworks, under the guise of studying "artistic tastes." The paintings were by two contemporary, abstract artists, Paul Klee and Wassily Kandinsk.

The students were divided into two groups, supposedly based on their preferences for each painting. They were only told that there were two groups and which group they had been assigned to. They were introduced to each other and then told which of the people they'd been introduced to belonged in each group. The real study began when they were then asked to give points to a range of students within their group and outside of their group.

The findings made it clear that people showed a strong favoritism to those they believed to be part of their "group" and awarded them more points compared to those they perceived to be out of their group. It didn't seem to matter that they had been grouped together over something arbitrary and unimportant.

This revealed a strong insight into the way our society works, and a very important social psychological process. Groups only exist because individuals perceive them to. Despite the fact that the students were grouped only a few minutes before awarding points, there was still the perception that a group had formed, causing in-group favoritism. They did not consider that they had no true connection to each other and no real reason to favor their group over the other. Once they had been given the impression that they belonged to one group instead of another, they instantly felt more favorably to their own group and less favorably to those not in their group.

This can be a very powerful advantage when utilized in real life. Though people have no solid reason to favor you, if you can make them believe you are both members of a group that separates you from others, you will cause some favoritism to be directed your way.

Some argue that it's hardwired into our evolutionary psychology. Imagine your ancestors roaming the grasslands of Africa hundreds of thousands of years ago. The in-group mentality would mean that someone would favor those they thought were in their family or social group, assisting them in finding food and keeping up their survival. Without this in-group preference, our ancestors wouldn't be able to pass on their genes to the next generation because they would be less likely to help those around them survive.

Hundreds of thousands of years later and most of us still have that instinct, to prefer those we think share something with us and are part of whatever group we may have created. Knowing that people operate this way means that you can use it to your benefit.

For example, if you were looking to hire someone to work at your company, and a potential candidate went to the same college as you, you would feel immediately more favorable toward them than before. Even if you hadn't met them yet, or you hadn't read their resumé, the mere fact that you both went to the same school would automatically give them a slight advantage in your mind.

If you know that someone shares something with you, whether it's that you both enjoy a certain music genre, or that you both worked in the same organization for a while, you can use this to your advantage and form a bond with someone who will lead others to favor you.

Try to create groups where you share similarities, inside jokes, and an appreciation of similar things and where you are all comfortable with one another. When you meet a stranger, all you have to do is mention a similarity that will liken you to them. Perhaps it's a physical attribute, something they're wearing, or some other personal detail about their life.

We can all relate to the excitement of the moment when someone mentions a detail and we can instantly say, "Me too!" This is related to the psychological concept of being attracted to similarity. When we find someone who is similar to us, or when we believe we share something with them, we immediately want to get to know them better and connect further. It's all about being able to share experiences and the excitement of knowing that someone has seen, felt, or experienced something that you have, too.

This creates a bond, no matter how small or irrelevant it seems. We all want to connect with others and even momentary connections like these will liken others to you. They can't help but lower their guard and be more open to you and the things that you are saying to them, because they see themselves in you.

It doesn't have to be a difficult or insightful similarity. If you're at a party and come across someone wearing a red shirt just like you are, you just need to state how you've both decided "it's redshirt day today," and an instant bond will form. You'll both smile at the revelation and this single piece of common ground can act as a springboard for mutual comfort. Everyone feels better and more comfortable around people who they know are similar to them or share commonalities.

You can't let it end there, though, as this is just the beginning. Once you've identified the starting ground of your similarities, you need to build upon this. Ask questions that may lead to further agreements. They don't have to be heavy, debatable questions, such as what their purpose in life is. Just light conversation about hobbies, jobs or interests is enough.

The more you have in common, the more psychologically comfortable the person you're speaking to will become. This is because they can't help but be drawn to someone they feel is a member of their in-group. It doesn't matter that a group hasn't been identified or formed in a concrete way. The person has already decided that you're not a complete and total stranger to them because they identify with you on some level.

Once they've lowered their guard, you can use the other techniques in this book to be even more likeable to them. The first step is establishing that bond of commonality and then building from there. Maybe they like the same kind of music you do. Maybe they went to the same school. It's very easy to develop any kind of commonality with people and keep a constant stream of conversation around this. Your main mission here is to try to get the person to look at you as less of an alien and more as a part of their in-group.

It's important to keep in mind that certain cultural groupings are more predisposed to this. Often those from America or Western Europe in general tend to be more individualistic and less taken in on group commonalities, requiring more effort for them to feel as if they're part of the in-group. Alternatively, Asian cultures, especially more traditional cultures, pay a high premium on alma mater, social organizations, churches or religious institutions, educational institutions, and so on down the line. Even geographic origin—for example, if your ancestors come from a specific province of China—can be a tremendous source of bonding.

By using this in-group versus out-group dynamic to your advantage, you can target something that is deeply ingrained in others and allow you to be more likeable to them without much effort. Sometimes it's the first step, the initial creation of common ground that is most important when building relationships. While certain cultures require a lot more prodding to trigger it, once triggered, it can be an instant and powerful source of likeability.

Chapter 7. A Simple Roadmap

In previous chapters, we've discussed some of the specific ways of thinking about social interactions that can make them more positive. Now we're going to get into some of the direct methods of socializing that will increase your likeability and help you to form better relationships with others.

One important thing to keep in mind is that, for the most part, people are self-absorbed to a fairly high degree. This is significant because it gives us predictability in how to deal with people. If you know what someone is looking for, and you possess the ability to give it to them, things will tend to go better in general. In this chapter, you'll find a roadmap of sorts to people's conscious and subconscious interests and desires that will tell you exactly how to act for social success—a roadmap to follow.

People Want to Talk About Themselves

Dale Carnegie, the famous author of the book *How to Win Friends and Influence People*, gave a lot of advice on self-improvement, salesmanship, speaking, and interpersonal skills over the course of his life. Much of his advice is now derided as common sense, even though the very reason it's so widespread is because of his book. Perhaps one of his best pieces of advice was simply to get people to talk, or even brag, about themselves, because this will make them enjoy conversing with you. He was quoted as saying, "You can make more friends in two months by becoming interested in other people than you can in two years by trying to get other people interested in you." Consequently, this is one of the most bandied about pieces of conversation advice.

But is there any evidence to back this up? As it turns out, there's plenty. A 2012 study conducted by neuroscientists Diana Tamir and Jason Mitchell at Harvard University comprising of five different brain-imaging experiments found our urge to share personal information with others is one of the most fundamental and powerful parts of being human. The brain images showed that sharing information about ourselves triggers the same sensations in our brains as we experience when we eat food and have sex—two behaviors that we are biologically compelled to do. Thus, it seems we are biologically compelled to share and communicate our thoughts.

Tamir and Mitchell first designed studies with the intention of observing and trying to somehow quantify the unusually high value that people placed on being able to share their thoughts and feelings. They then recruited dozens of volunteers—the majority of which were Americans who lived near the Harvard campus—and questioned them about themselves as well as topics unrelated to them.

One method that the researchers implemented to determine how much the participants valued being able to talk about themselves was to offer a modest financial incentive to anybody who would answer questions about other people instead. Some of the questions involved casual subjects about hobbies and personal tastes, while others were about personality traits, such as intelligence, curiosity, or aggression. The researchers found that many of the participants were willing to pass up on the money, preferring the rewarding feelings of self-disclosure over financial gain. In fact, the average participant willingly gave up between 17% and 25% of their possible earnings just so that they could reveal personal information.

Moreover, Tamir and Mitchell used a functional magnetic resonance imaging scanner (fMRI) to observe what parts of the brain were most excited when the subjects were talking about themselves. Generally, they found a correlation between self-disclosure and heightened activity in brain regions belonging to the mesolimbic dopamine system—again, the same region that's associated with the rewarding and satisfying feeling we get from food, money, and sex.

That means that each party in a conversation or social setting is highly incentivized to talk about themselves from a neurochemical perspective. Dale Carnegie was in fact correct. How can we utilize this knowledge for our social success?

The most important step for most will be to start imposing limits on themselves. Yes, it feels good to talk about yourself as the studies have shown, but when you do so, you are depriving others the space and time to talk about themselves. And in the end, the goal of social intelligence is to make yourself more likable, not necessarily to feel better about social interaction.

Talking about yourself to some extent is natural, both biologically and within the flow of a conversation. It's estimated that some 40%

of what we say relates to expressing our own thoughts and feelings, and that's because it is highly rewarding to do so. Therefore, you must carefully balance your own disclosures with allowing others to speak freely.

This comes in two approaches. First, be cognizant of the types of self-disclosure you typically make. This is to ensure you are receiving the rewarding feelings from disclosure without being annoyingly self-absorbed.

When you talk a lot about yourself, it often comes across as over-the-top, immodest, highly competitive, or even thoughtless. While you may believe that you are just being proud, or even that you are using self-disclosure simply to make conversation, you have to be mindful of how others might perceive it. When you talk about yourself in an extremely positive way, you can be labeled a bragger, and if you do the opposite and talk about yourself negatively, you might come across as lacking confidence or just being a downer.

Generally speaking, people want to be entertained, so when you do talk about yourself you'll be more socially successful if you can tell interesting stories instead of constantly blurting out "I think…" and "I feel…" without any thought toward how it will be received. If people aren't speaking, they want to hear something they are interested in.

More than that, though, use people's inherent desire to talk about themselves as a mechanism for achieving social success by consciously allowing everyone else to talk more. Be curious about others, ask them questions that give them the opportunity to brag, and generally let the conversation focus on them. Concentrate on their strengths and allow them to paint themselves in a positive light, being aware of false modesty and reinforcing praise in those moments. Be a good listener, show genuine curiosity and interest in the conversation, and encourage them to continue talking about themselves.

When's the last time you asked someone five questions in a row without interrupting or interjecting with your own anecdote? What about ten questions? This is the exact type of interaction that feels good to people that we routinely deny them of because we can't resist our own temptation. It's easy to do this in a way that doesn't devolve into an interview—just stay on the same topic and keep digging deeper.

At the bottom of all of this is the essential skill of being an attentive and active listener. We all have the potential within us to become better listeners—it just takes focus and awareness.

Focus on Similarity

It's certainly true that one of the easiest ways to connect with people is through similarities you share with them.

We naturally like socializing with similar people because it comes with a sense of comfort and familiarity, so we know what to expect. We feel safe. Not surprisingly, there have been countless studies over the years demonstrating the different ways in which we are more attracted to people whom we see as having similar personality traits to us.

A 1985 study by Lewak, Wakefield, and Briggs showed that participants were more drawn to others of similar intelligence. This makes sense because somebody who struggles to understand complex intellectual topics likely won't enjoy talking about or be interested in those subjects, and somebody whose biggest passions are intellectual pursuits likely wants to discuss their ideas with others who are curious and interested.

The further apart you get on any spectrum, the harder it will be to find some middle ground that satisfies both sides. This is true for parties with opposing beliefs and attitudes, but it can also be true for people with vastly different personality traits. If you want to take an efficient and sustainable route to social success, you should focus a majority of your time interacting with people who have similar personality traits to yourself because they will like and respect you more right off the bat.

Another study, this one by Morell, Twillman, and Sullaway in 1989, showed that we are more romantically attracted to people with the same personality type as ourselves. So a person with a Type A personality—hard-driving, competitive, conscious of time, etc.—will likely prefer dating a partner who also has a Type A personality. Those with Type B traits—relaxed, lower-stress, reflective, etc.—will likewise prefer others with Type B personalities when it comes to romantic relationships.

And this trend doesn't just apply to initial attraction. One study by Caspi and Herbener in 1990—and another by Lazarus in 2001—showed that in the case of long-term relationships and marriages, similar personality traits proved to be an accurate predictor of a couple's stability and happiness.

The notion that "opposites attract" is especially common to mention when it comes to relationships, but the evidence from psychological studies provides a solid contradiction to that notion. If you're after more successful relationships, then similarity with your partner seems like the way to go. And this makes plenty of sense—somebody who's highly ambitious and career-oriented might judge a more relaxed person as being lazy, while the supposedly lazy person might wish that their partner would stress less and take more time to enjoy life. Neither partner is right or wrong, but the more they have to compromise in order to be together, the greater the likelihood of relationship complications.

Generally speaking, the more different you are from your partner, the more effort and communication will be required to have a successful relationship. If both partners are capable of consistently being open and working through differences, you can still have a rewarding and successful relationship where your differences are a benefit to one another. However, if you're looking for a partner who's extremely different from you so that you can "balance each other out," you may want to rethink that strategy.

But what about non-romantic relationships? Can friends get along well if they have clashing personality traits?

In 2004, a team of five psychologists conducted a study that showed that the preference extends beyond romantic interest and includes friendships and relationships with family members as well. The study subjects were significantly more likely to spend time hanging out with people who had mostly similar personality traits to themselves (Nangle, Erdley, Zeff, Stanchfield, and Gold). If you are a goal-oriented and hard-working individual, for example, you'll more than likely gravitate toward friends who are the same way.

Donn Byrne and his colleagues conducted two studies, one in 1968 and the other in 1971, that demonstrated that our attraction to similar people goes beyond personality traits and into things such as political views, religious beliefs, and other attitudes and affiliations. In fact, they showed that common attitudes and likability are directly related to each other as represented by a linear function, meaning that the more similar attitudes and beliefs you share with somebody, the more you will like them. Therefore, we are about two times more likely to like somebody with whom we agree on 8 out of 10 issues relative to somebody with whom we only agree on 4 out of 10 issues.

Of course, this phenomenon isn't just applicable to *positive* beliefs and attitudes. Sharing hatred for the same thing can also bring people together because, as the saying goes, "the enemy of my enemy is my friend."

Sports fanaticism provides a perfect example of this, as it's extremely common to see fans of different teams come together to root against the reviled perennial champions of their given sport. And while building a new friendship through a common hate for a sports team is relatively harmless, unfortunately, this human tendency to unite over common hatred can have more serious negative implications for other attitudes and beliefs, as is often the case in political and religious conflicts.

The similarity and attraction theory doesn't even end there, however. It's actually been shown that having a similar name as somebody else also increases the probability that the other person will like you. That being the case, you can try to give yourself a nickname similar to your peers if you want to improve your likeability that extra little bit.

Ultimately, what all of these studies show is that the old adage "birds of a feather flock together" is a lot more accurate than "opposites attract" when it comes to human relationships. And you'll likely find this to be the case if you reflect on your own social history and current relationships. It wouldn't be surprising if some of your oldest and closest friends are the ones whom you have the most in common with, while some of those relationship failures and friends with whom you lost touch were less similar and therefore less compatible with you.

So what can you do in order to take advantage of this knowledge?

The obvious answer is to emphasize your similarities and downplay your differences as much as possible when you interact with people. Some of your relationships may be deep and span a wide ridge of mutual interests, while others might hinge on one or two shared traits or interests. Whatever the case may be, you'll maximize your social success by focusing on what you have in common with people.

Suppose that you're an American who has never really cared much for soccer, but you're going to be moving to a country in Europe or South America where soccer is a big deal. You might still find the sport itself boring, but learning about it and developing an interest for it can give you an easy conversation starter with a massive percentage of the population in your new home. You'll find it much easier to make friends in any situation if you can talk to people about the things that they're passionate about. The goal is to find common ground, and that doesn't always come effortlessly.

Once the initial similarity is established, you simply stand a far better chance of overall social acceptance, and sometimes that is all we can hope for.

On that note, being naturally curious and interested in many things enables you to connect with a more diverse and overall greater number of people. If you spend all of your free time watching TV, you won't have the same ability or number of opportunities to connect with people as somebody who has a lot of hobbies and interests that they actively pursue in their free time. You can make yourself more *interesting* just by being more *interested.*

So let people talk about themselves. Let them brag to their heart's desire! Be a curious listener, and as you listen, you can develop an understanding for what shared traits and interests make you closer with any given individual, and which ones will separate you.

Focus on the positives you share with people as you allow them to express their thoughts and feelings to you and you'll have many successful relationships as a result.

Chapter 8. Emotional Calibration

How do you connect with people and what makes a connection deep and powerful?

Some of our strongest connections are formed when we are able to be empathetic—that is, to understand and even share in the feelings of another person. Being able to relate to people by understanding how you affect them and what else they are affected by can enable you to build close and intimate relationships with others through more personal communication with them.

When friends are experiencing difficult times and negative emotions, it's often simply a listening ear and an empathetic shoulder to cry on that can bring them the greatest comfort and relief.

The Power of Vulnerability

If there's one part of empathy that is crucial relative to all the others, it's probably vulnerability. The ability to make yourself vulnerable is what allows you to present yourself in an accessible way to others, and that in turn is what enables them to get past whatever shame and fear they may have and to express what they truly think and feel.

Brené Brown delivered a TED Talk on vulnerability in 2010 that has since been viewed over 30 million times and has been the catalyst of the whole "vulnerability" movement. In Brown's talk, she tells her own story of learning to be vulnerable, and how accepting that undesirable feeling enabled her to experience more compassion, joy, and love in her life.

Being vulnerable often means being the first person to admit flaws and weaknesses. Therefore, it is often the people with the most confidence and self-esteem who are willing to be the most vulnerable. These are the people who are at peace with where they are in life, and who consistently act with integrity and grace based on their core beliefs and values. When you have that feeling of self-worthiness, you can experience vulnerability in a truly positive way, where you are okay with your flaws and weaknesses because they are just a natural part of being human.

We all make mistakes from time to time; it's how you handle mistakes that most impacts social success. Researchers who published a study in the American Psychology Association found that taking ownership and accountability for mistakes rather than making excuses or deflecting blame makes you more attractive. Leaders who take responsibility for mistakes gain the trust and respect of their colleagues, while individuals who do so on a personal level can form healthier relationships with others as they trust that disagreements and adversity can be overcome.

There is actually a widely accepted theory in social psychology known as the pratfall effect, which—counterintuitive as it may seem—actually states that making certain kinds of mistakes makes you more likable because you are relatable in your vulnerability. Also referred to as the blemishing effect, this phenomenon has been tested and confirmed many times over, and remembering it can help you to feel better in times of embarrassment or shame.

One simple example of the pratfall effect's validity is that people tend to like a person who clumsily trips on video more than those who don't trip in the video. When we feel embarrassed, it's natural to assume that others might like us less because we like ourselves a bit less in those moments. But if we don't take ourselves too seriously in those moments and bear them with a smile, it can even be endearing to others.

As further proof that perfection is overrated, the University of Chicago Press published a study in 2011 by psychologists Danit Ein-Gar, Baba Shiv, and Zakary Tormala, which showed that transparently adding a small dose of negative information to an otherwise positive product description actually made the product more appealing and credible.

The researchers walked around a college campus and approached students to offer them a chocolate bar that was advertised as chilled, favored by consumers on a taste test, and available at a discounted price because it had a piece that was broken, which could be seen through the transparent wrapper. They approached two groups of students—some who were distracted by an upcoming exam that day, and others who were walking leisurely around the campus.

The results of the study were clear. The students who were part of the leisurely and undistracted experimental group were twice as likely to purchase the bar after being told that it was discounted because it was broken, while those from the group who had an upcoming exam were half as likely to purchase the chocolate bar. The researchers concluded that negative information can enhance positive disposition toward a product as long as it is processed effortlessly, which has some interesting implications for our social lives.

If people think of others in the same way that they think of an imperfect chocolate bar, that would indicate that being vulnerable and transparently owning a mistake can make others see you more favorably than if you didn't make a mistake in the first place.

There are a few major conclusions that we can draw from this.

If you are vulnerable and show a crack in your armor but handle it maturely, that will increase your likelihood of social success because it shows that you are honest and genuine. Additionally, making mistakes just makes you appear more human, and that, in turn, makes you more likeable. People who appear perfect can seem threatening, but people who are transparent about their imperfections are safer and thus easier to like. On the other hand, nobody is perfect, and so covering up vulnerabilities is ultimately unattractive because it's inherently manipulative and dishonest.

Perhaps most importantly, people who are willing to be vulnerable don't pay attention to judgment from others, and they don't judge others for their vulnerabilities, either. Being judgmental makes people feel on edge and defensive when they are around you, which is decidedly counterproductive for achieving social success.

If you ever find yourself making conclusions about somebody's character over one trait or one mistake, you are passing judgment and should try to think in a different way. For example, when you learn of somebody committing a crime, instead of saying that person is bad, simply say that they did a bad thing. Good people mess up all the time, and holding others to a standard of perfection will make you less desirable company, yourself.

When you put all of those things together and you allow yourself to be vulnerable, you show supreme confidence. You put yourself fully out there, shortcomings and all, and you say that it's okay to be fallible—actually, it's even more charming and attractive. The key is to react maturely and avoid getting defensive whenever you do make a mistake. So the next time you make an error at work that costs the company time and money to correct, go straight to your manager and take full responsibility while reinforcing that you'll correct the mistake going forward. If your manager is a good leader, they may trust you even more as a result of how you handled your mistake.

In a more general sense, what can you do to be more vulnerable? Be aware of your personal weaknesses and be willing to admit them. When you make mistakes, acknowledge them, apologize to the people who are affected, admit your limitations, and, when appropriate, make fun of yourself and use self-deprecating humor to ease tension and discomfort. Moreover, when you feel jealousy, envy, or simple admiration for others, admit that. It may make them feel good while removing the burden from you that comes with bottling those things up.

For example, if you have a friend who is more successful than you and seems to have the life that you want, you can express that positively by saying, "I envy your life and admire the way that you've built it. I hope that you can have a positive influence on me so that I can achieve the same success." Envy and especially jealousy can often be ugly emotions, but if you express them positively rather than hiding them, you'll be more likeable and socially successful as a result.

On that note, vulnerability and likeability really do seem to go hand in hand. So practice some self-compassion, build your self-esteem, and open up about your shortcomings. Like Brené Brown, you may find that you live a fuller and happier life as a result.

Social Calibration

We can step into other people's shoes with empathy, but what about adapting your personality based on the company you're keeping at a given time?

This adaptability, or "social calibration," simply means being able to refine the attitudes and behaviors that you portray based on the present crowd. People who are highly socially calibrated can find a way to put their best and most charming foot forward in a wide variety of different social interactions by matching the tonality, opinions, and energy of their audience.

Social calibration, therefore, isn't just what you say, but how you say it and how you present yourself in general—encompassing everything from facial expressions and hand gestures to tonality and vocabulary. The key difference between social calibration and people pleasing is that somebody who is socially calibrated remains authentically themselves through all of the various circumstances, only making minor tweaks to the way they portray themselves so that their interactions run more smoothly.

For example, somebody who is socially calibrated and likes to joke around a lot may tell dirty or mature jokes with their friends, toned-down versions while at work, and entirely different and less-mature jokes to or around kids. Their sense of humor is present in all three scenarios but it's emphasized in a different way based on the circumstances of the people who are hearing the jokes.

Being highly socially calibrated requires a good deal of self-awareness—knowing how you act and paying attention to how other people react to you. You can't properly calibrate yourself to an audience if you don't at least have a general understanding of that audience's typical social behavior. Likewise, you have to calibrate to other circumstances such as location and atmosphere—you wouldn't behave the same way at an expensive restaurant as you would at a college bar.

It's important to make the distinction between calibration and manipulation because being socially well-calibrated is really a means of being socially successful as your authentic self, not a way to change who you are. It all comes down to understanding how another person or group will receive our personality or our "message," and trying to portray that in a language/manner that is easily understood and relatable. This actually prevents us from stepping on toes, being misunderstood, or having our "message" rejected—not for its contents—but because of *how* it was conveyed.

What happens when you aren't socially well-calibrated?

Well, you aren't able to read and respond to social cues effectively, which can potentially come off as "awkward," "weird," or even "creepy." Most circumstances and social situations come with some socially accepted way to behave, and venturing outside of what is socially acceptable often has negative consequences.

We all know somebody about whom it's said, "You can't take them anywhere." That's the person who sometimes makes others feel shame and embarrassment just by association because they don't act in socially acceptable ways in public.

Likewise, you've probably met somebody who manages to put others at ease in tense situations or get others to be excited or aroused when the energy was low. That's what being highly socially calibrated is about—being able to read a situation and adapt on the fly to get the most social benefit given the circumstances.

So what can you do to increase your social calibration?

First, focus on being observant and understanding social context. Then think to yourself about what behavior is appropriate in that context. As you socialize, measure how people react to you and others, and conform (not a bad thing here) to the behavior that is best-received. At the same time, realize that social cues and hints are often very subtle, and it takes work to become better calibrated, so don't beat yourself up when you do make mistakes or read a situation poorly. Analyze the mistake, learn from it, and then move on and continue socializing.

Let's say, for example, that you're in a social group with a close friend and a few strangers. If you and your friend have a playful relationship, you might engage in some harsh ribbing of your friend if given the opportunity. But what if the strangers become obviously uncomfortable when you do? Well, just as the strangers may not realize that you're just kidding around with your close friend, you may not realize that they don't have any of those types of relationships and that it isn't normal to them. You can learn to recognize that the atmosphere wasn't casual enough for that to be appropriate and that you didn't understand the rest of your audience enough to know how they would react. In the future, you'll wait to get a better feel for the situation before doing something that might make others uncomfortable.

Being socially well-calibrated will enable you to have positive relationships with a wide variety of different people, and it will help you quickly make new friends or integrate yourself into new social groups.

Emotional Intelligence

In the same vein as social calibration, we have what's known as emotional intelligence—the capability to use the information you recognize about your own and other people's emotions and feelings in order to guide your thinking and behavior. Similarly, with social calibration, you are reading people and being aware of the subtext in social situations so that you can adjust your own emotions and adapt to your circumstances to achieve your desired outcome.

Somebody who is highly emotionally intelligent can easily analyze and understand other people's emotions and intentions, enabling them to have more positive and smooth relationships.

There are some things you can do to increase—or rather practice—emotional intelligence.

One of the most effective ways to do this is to read fiction and try to guess what people are thinking and feeling and the root causes of those feelings based on how the storyline has affected them. Both for characters and for people you actually interact with, think like a detective and consider the motivations and intentions behind their actions. Personally, you can mindfully manage your emotional highs and lows and try to understand them, rather than just feeling and reacting to them.

When you put all of these social skills together—vulnerability, social calibration, and emotional intelligence—you'll be prepared to succeed in practically every social situation. You'll be able to form deep and intimate relationships with the people you like best, and you'll be able to accurately and genuinely convey who you are and what your "message" is to all of the people whom you interact with. Understanding and awareness of yourself and those around you are truly the fundamentals of attaining the fulfilling social life that you desire.

Chapter 9. Traits for Social Catastrophe

In the first eight chapters of this book, we've talked all about how to be socially successful. Now it's time to learn about what can make you a social catastrophe so that you can avoid the mistakes that could make everything you've learned so far go to waste. Regardless of how charming you are, there are some social habits and traits that can make your personality off-putting and drive people away from you. This chapter will tell you what those habits and traits are, how to avoid them, and the social cost that comes with them.

A reassuring message that you should take away from this book is that being socially successful doesn't require you to be extremely outgoing, entertaining, funny, or charismatic. You can make yourself an above-average socializer by doing two things that everybody is capable of doing: actively and curiously listening so that people enjoy talking to you, and getting rid of any offensive characteristics you may have so that people enjoy being around you. If you do those two things, you'll be well on your way already.

Don't Hide Your Emotions

People like authenticity, plain and simple. If you hide your emotions or fail to appear forthcoming, you will lower your odds of forming new relationships and thus decrease your social success. This is similar to vulnerability, where people value those who can bare their souls and embrace their flaws. Similarly, people like to feel that they are getting to see the real you without any filters or ulterior motives.

Psychologists Allison Tackman and Sanjay Srivastava conducted a study in which they measured participants' reactions to other people's emotional suppression. They did this by videotaping people as they watched two movie scenes—one sexually arousing scene and one sad one. The viewers were instructed to either react as they naturally would to the scenes or to suppress their emotions. College students then watched the viewers as they reacted to the videos and were subsequently asked how interested they would be in befriending the people in the videos and what they thought of the viewers' personalities in general.

The results showed that the viewers who had suppressed their emotional responses were perceived as less likeable, less extroverted, and less agreeable than those who had reacted naturally. The researchers concluded that this was likely to do with reciprocation, saying, "People… do not pursue close relationships indiscriminately—they probably look for people who are likely to reciprocate their investments. So when perceivers detect that someone is hiding their emotions, they may interpret that as a disinterest in the things that emotional expression facilitates—closeness, social support, and interpersonal coordination."

What does that mean for us? The major takeaway is that honesty, vulnerability, and being genuine in how you express your emotions will make you more likeable. In romantic relationships, for example, mutual attraction and shared interests usually only go so far. When you grow comfortable enough to open up to each other—to filter and hide your feelings less—your attraction can turn into love. Deep friendships are the same way. Being genuine and expressing how you really feel makes other people feel more comfortable doing the same, and everybody feels better when they are able to be their genuine selves.

If you're on board with the benefits of being expressive but just don't know how to do so naturally, start with three things: hand gestures, facial expressions, and vocal inflection. Show how you feel honestly and often. With those three strategies, you don't have to change what you say at all to become a more expressive communicator and, therefore, to seem more genuine and honest so that people will trust and like you more.

Don't Be Too Nice or Accommodating

How you treat others plays a big part in how they will treat you in return—we all know that. People like to be treated with respect. What may be a bit less obvious, however, is that there is such thing as being too nice to people, to the point that it actually becomes a detriment to your likeability.

Researchers at Washington State University conducted a study in 2010 that examined how people felt about others who went above and beyond to be nice to them. College students participated in a game in which they were given "points" that they could either give up or redeem for meal-service vouchers. The participants were broken up into groups of five, and they were told that giving up their points as individuals would increase their odds of winning a monetary prize for their group.

Unbeknownst to the volunteers, four members of every five-person group were actually actors, many of who were instructed to give up many of their points and only claim a few vouchers. The researchers actually found that the real participants didn't like being in a group with these extra-nice teammates, either because the teammate's unselfishness made them feel bad, or because they suspected ulterior motives—a bigger share of the monetary reward, perhaps.

Applying what we learned from this game to our real lives, the lesson is that you don't want to be the person who *always* goes out of their way to accommodate others. It's perfectly acceptable to say no sometimes, so long as you explain why you can't commit—even if that explanation is that you would rather spend your time and energy doing other things. Obviously, that doesn't mean that you should be rude or put others down; simply explain in a nice way that the time is valuable to you and you'd be better served doing something else. If you are too nice, you become incredibly suspicious, people put their guards up, and you are left out in the cold.

The goal is to find a healthy balance between assertiveness and accommodation and to prioritize yourself above other people more often than the other way around. When you're *too* nice, you may think that others will see you as generous and unselfish, but quite often you'll actually be making them feel uncomfortable, suspicious, or anxious instead.

Of course, you shouldn't just stop being nice altogether. Simply keep in mind that it's wise to try to ease people's discomfort when you do nice things for them by qualifying the nice things with a reason.

For example, if you have a friend who needs a ride across the city and you want to be nice and drive them, doing so out of pure generosity might make your friend feel bad. Instead, for example, you can say that it's no extra trouble, as you were planning to run an errand in that part of town anyway and you can just drop them off on your way. You should always keep in mind that people operate under the assumption that nothing in life—not even an act of kindness—comes free. So when you are being nice, be able to provide an explanation as to why your accommodation isn't free even if, in reality, it is.

For many of you who are reading this, thinking more about if you are, in fact, *too* nice may be necessary. If you make a constant effort to go out of your way for others and sometimes feel angry or upset that people don't go out of their way for you, then you may not be acting out of genuine kindness at all—even if you think that you are. It's becoming an all too common phenomenon in modern society for people to use "niceness" as a manipulation to get others to like them or to make others indebted to them, and many of the manipulators in this scenario don't realize what they're even doing. If that might be you, becoming more aware of that habit and changing it can completely change your social life in a positive way.

The real key here is to put yourself first and make sure that you are healthy with all of your needs taken care of before you make sacrifices to accommodate others so that you can be sure that those accommodations you make for others come from a sincere desire to be helpful and not from ulterior motives.

A good analogy is how flight attendants instruct passengers before takeoff that, in the event of an emergency, they should secure their own oxygen masks before helping others. You can become a socially successful person while still being helpful and accommodating, but only so long as you are taking care of yourself first.

The Power of Eye Contact

Surely, you've heard many times before that eye contact is important. In terms of social success, the importance of eye contact isn't so much in the act itself as it is in all the things that we assume about people depending on how good or bad at it they are.

People who don't make eye contact are often thought of as untrustworthy or deceitful, two things that can be very harmful in how people perceive you. While scientific studies haven't found those correlations to actually be true, the assumption persists nonetheless, and thus you should remember to make eye contact if you want to avoid being thought of in that way.

Moreover, there is a truly significant number of positive assumptions that we make about people who make eye contact that can surely improve people's perception of you. Generally, people who make eye contact are seen as more dominant and powerful; more warm and personable; more attractive and likeable; more qualified, skilled, competent, and valuable; more trustworthy, honest, and since; and more confident and emotionally stable. In other words, just about all the things that are associated with social success.

Elisabeth von dem Hagen, a psychologist on the UK's Medical Research Council, used functional magnetic resonance imagery scanners (fMRI) to study what happens in our brains when we are making eye contact. She found that eye contact activated regions of the "social brain," including the area where the temporal lobe in the side of the brain joins the parietal lobe above it, the frontal lobe near the midline, and the region where the visual cortex receives signals from the retina. This means that the occurrence of eye contact, or direct gaze, literally changes our perception of others on a biological level.

As we are increasingly more caught up in a battle for our attention between our phones and our real-life conversation partners, the ability to make eye contact has become an especially powerful tool. When you can avoid breaking your gaze and show somebody that they have your undivided attention, you can effectively win them over and enhance their perception of you.

When you fail to make good eye contact or deliberately avoid it, on the other hand, you risk that your conversation partners will feel hurt and their sense of belonging will be diminished—a feeling captured perfectly by the German expression "wie Luft behandeln," which translates as "to be looked at as though air." Psychologists demonstrated this phenomenon by subjecting a random passerby to "wie Luft behandeln" as they walked around a college campus. Afterwards, the researchers interviewed the unfortunate subjects, who often reported that they felt disconnected from others after the experience.

So what can you do to improve your eye contact? First, understand the difference between gazing (good) and staring (bad), because you can easily come across as weird or creepy if your eye contact is too intense. Additionally, learn to become comfortable with tension. Holding eye contact may require fighting your instincts at first, but it is an important part of socializing, so you should learn to overcome any habits of looking away when you meet somebody's gaze if that's something that you typically do.

Finally, you can remember the general guidelines for what amount of eye contact is appropriate—50% when talking and 75% when listening. When you speak, you want others to be comfortable having their attention on you, but you also want to make sure that you don't appear to be hiding something or feeling uncomfortable yourself. And as you listen, you want whoever is speaking to see that you are engaged, but you don't want to look at them so much that they might feel creeped out. As long as you are in the general ballpark of 50% and 75% for speaking and listening, respectively, you'll be making the most out of the surprisingly powerful tool of eye contact.

Sometimes, the first step to becoming successful at anything is just diminishing or eliminating the bad habits that you developed when you were less knowledgeable and experienced.

You may have gotten in trouble whenever you were emotional as a child so that now you always bottle those things up and remain relatively expressionless. Likewise, you may have learned in your childhood that the best way to get your needs met at that vulnerable age was to be extremely nice and accommodating to people. Furthermore, making the right amount of eye contact is something that simply doesn't come naturally to a lot of people, especially those who tend to be shy.

Whatever your particular bad habits may be, accept that you have them and work on steadily improving them in the future.

If you aren't expressive, make the effort to be mindful in the moments that you feel strong emotions and just allow yourself to let it out. Even if nobody's around to see it, you can get more comfortable with your emotions so that you'll be able to start expressing them more when you are in an actual social situation. If you are always overly nice and accommodating, practice saying no sometimes and you'll probably realize that people don't think anything less of you for it if you prioritize yourself first. And if eye contact with strangers or even friends is difficult for you, then just consciously start ramping up how long you hold people's gazes until you do become comfortable.

You can make leaps and bounds of progress in terms of social success just by reducing how many off-putting habits and characteristics you have. That's often the best place to start.

Chapter 10. The Interconnected World

No guide to creating social success would be complete without taking into account that our social standing is often affected by factors out of our control—it is not solely a result of our own actions. The world is interconnected, and so we have to consider the people and circumstances around us as well as how we are perceived by others in order to use this knowledge about social science to our full advantage.

With the advent of social media, the ways that we are connecting with each other are being constantly reshaped by the technology we are developing. But while the mediums that we use to facilitate our interactions have changed, our thoughts and social behavior have remained much the same. Understanding the fundamentals of network effects, therefore, will remain a valuable social skill for a long time to come.

Word of Mouth Marketing

The science of social success and marketing quite often go hand in hand, as advertisers constantly seek to improve the ways that they target and sell to prospective consumers in much the same way we seek to improve how we present ourselves to others.

Word of mouth marketing (WOM) refers to the voluntary spread of a constructive marketing message from one person to another. It remains, to this day, the most effective form of advertising there is—and therefore one of the most effective means of getting others to open up to you socially as well. WOM is happening in all of our interactions, from in-person conversations to email and social media. Whenever we are considering buying a new product, we naturally trust opinions and reviews on that product if they come from sources we know and trust much more than if we see them as anonymous ads. Even if you want to try a new restaurant, your first instinct might be to ask a friend for their opinion or look up recent reviews online.

Just how valuable is word of mouth and recommendations from friends and family? Consider this—a recent Nielsen Global survey asked participants to rate their level of trust in a number of various marketing methods, including text and banner ads, magazine ads, and television ads. Of those surveyed, a whopping 92% of consumers reported that they would trust earned media such as WOM above all other marketing methods.

This is a big deal, but what does it mean for our social success? Quite simply, it means that the best way to grow your social network and to build new relationships is through word of mouth from the people who know you. People listen to their friends, and if the WOM on you is positive, people won't question it.

Suppose you go to a party where you don't know anybody, and you're on top of your social game and make a few new connections. No matter how charming or friendly you were, the amount that those new acquaintances trust you is going to be strongly limited by the fact that they've only known you for a day. But now imagine that you had an old friend at the party who knows you well and can speak to your character and also knows the other guests. Now that friend can give their trusted recommendation of you to the other party guests, and the odds of you seeing those people again and actually becoming friends with them increases dramatically.

Ultimately, the reason that word of mouth works as a way of marketing not just products, but people, comes down to something called social proof—the phenomenon in which people will replicate how they see others behaving in a given social situation, assuming that it's the correct way to act.

Robert Cialdini—one of the most respected psychologists in the field of influence and persuasion—considers social proof to be an essential factor of social success. When people can talk to somebody who has known you for an extended period of time and can speak to your character, that serves as social validation and relieves you of the burden of having to prove your character over time in order to gain the trust of new acquaintances.

In 2008, Cialdini and two of his colleagues—Goldstein and Griskevicius—conducted a study to illustrate the power of social proof by creating a perceived social norm and testing its effects on unknowing guests at a hotel. The experiment's goal was to measure the difference in guest compliance for two signs that encouraged reusing towels to lessen the environmental burden of washing them—one sign that appealed to social norms and one that didn't.

The original sign read, "Help save the environment. You can show your respect for nature and help save the environment by reusing your towels during your stay." The sign that attempted to utilize social proof said, "Join your fellow guests in helping to save the environment. Almost 75% of guests who are asked to participate in our new resource savings program do help by using their towels more than once. You can join your fellow guests in this program to help save the environment by reusing your towels during your stay."

In the rooms that had the original signs, 35% of the guests opted to hang their towels indicating that they would reuse them. In the rooms that had signs implying social proof, however, 44% of the guests agreed and hung their towels up for re-use.

The idea behind this is that people are attuned to how others behave in a given situation, and so when we see "proof" that many other people are already acting in a certain way, we often follow suit because we think that we should act in the same way. Keep in mind that a sign in a hotel room bathroom is a rather weak form of social proof, as it requires guests to notice and pay attention to it, while also lacking any true "proof" of seeing or hearing others who have participated. And even so, simply saying that people were participating caused a 9% increase in true participation of the guests—a significant difference for what is a weak application of social proof relative to word of mouth.

In marketing, the ability to create or enhance somebody's perception that you provide a valuable good or service by using social proof is undoubtedly effective. But the influence and persuasiveness of social proof is the same regardless of purpose, meaning that it can be applied effectively in our personal lives as well. As stated earlier in the case of a party where you don't know anybody versus one where you have a friend who knows others, you will like somebody better if they are endorsed by a good friend—essentially using word of mouth "marketing" to become more socially successful.

So how can you make the most of the persuasiveness created by social proof and the word of mouth phenomenon? That's up to your friends to some extent, as they are the ones who can "advertise" or endorse you to other people they know. You can ask your friends to talk you up and to speak to your positive characteristics, as well as any accomplishments and interests of yours that might make you seem interesting or cool to others. Make it known that you will do the same with them as often as possible.

That being said, depending on your friends, you understandably may feel a bit awkward just asking them to talk you up in a straightforward way. There will likely still be plenty of opportunities to take advantage of their endorsements more subtly, however.

For example, if your friend casually mentions another friend of theirs that you might like to meet or become friends with, you can take an interest in that person and mention to your friend some reasons that they sound like somebody you would get along well with. That in itself may be enough to get the ball rolling, as your friend will probably then tell their friend about you and how you became interested in them, which will take advantage of the reciprocity of liking principle from Chapter 6 as well as word of mouth marketing of you from your friend.

First impressions really are crucial when it comes to expanding your social network and increasing your social success, and word of mouth is all about making a great first impression on people before you even meet them. There is power in numbers, so when we see that a lot of people like somebody, we assume that they can't all be wrong, and so we naturally like that person, too. That's why mutual friends have been and will continue to be the best means of making positive new connections with people.

If you want to create social proof for yourself on an everyday basis, a good place to start is by taking an interest in what your close friends are doing, and trying to network through them. Use your friends as stepping stones as often as possible. For example, if you have a friend who is part of a book club and has made a lot of friends through that, you might read one of the books and tag along to a meeting. Because you already have a friend in the group, you should find it easier to make other friends and thus expand your social network. Ultimately, if you implement the lessons from this book and develop your social skills, you'll naturally get more social proof.

Stay Positive (on Social Media)

Social media is everywhere. It's not often that you go through a day where social media isn't involved. This is not always a bad thing. Social media has the power to connect us all, especially when staying in touch can be so difficult. The power of the interconnected world is probably best demonstrated through social media. However, there are also some adverse effects as well.

A famous study of Facebook usage by Ethan Kross in 2013 studied the effect of Facebook on the overall happiness and satisfaction of a group of participants. Eighty-two subjects were text messaged five times each day for two weeks to examine how Facebook usage influenced how they felt. The result was that they tended to be a lot more depressed than average members of the population. But this isn't due to anything about Facebook itself. It isn't the mechanics or the software; it's the content that is the real issue.

The research suggested that when you are engaging in high levels of social activity, like being on Facebook for a long time, you become more aware of others and how their lives compare to yours. People who reported negative feelings regarding their social media were mostly distraught because they felt that their lives weren't as exciting as those of their Facebook friends.

This isn't really hard to believe. Every time you get on Facebook, there may be countless photos of friends and family travelling, partying, and having so many experiences that you may not have. It's hard not to compare when faced with these realities and feel that you're not living life to the fullest.

In many cases, these people who seem to be living such full lives aren't even friends at all. They could be just casual acquaintances, or people from high school that you haven't seen or spoken to in years and only keep up with via Facebook.

However, people tend to focus on their achievements and how they compare to their own. Instead of allowing yourself to feel happy for the person that bought a multi-million-dollar house, you have feelings of envy and jealousy. Eventually, these feelings fester into being depressed and unfulfilled with how your life is going.

The release of this study was shocking to people around the world, confirming suspicions that people already had. However, the study also had a second point that was just as important as the first.

When participants divided their Facebook updates on what they chose to receive while blocking the rest, there was a much better outcome. It seemed that these people who filtered their Facebook feeds to receive only positive news, or news that wouldn't sadden them, tended to be much happier and more positive people.

The researchers stated that if you used Facebook in a thoughtful and focused way, paying attention to only the positive or uplifting posts, you would be less likely to become depressed. People tended to be much happier and more optimistic when choosing to only receive positive information.

This is a wide-scale example of emotional contagion. It's not difficult to believe that emotions are contagious and easily spread from one person to another. We know that when we're surrounded by happy people, we are more likely to respond in the same manner. This works for the reverse as well.

In terms of Facebook, it's clear that when people choose to only receive positive information, they will simply feel motivated. This is something that can very easily be used to your advantage. If you know that negative information will have a negative impact on you, then the simple solution is to stop negative information. You need to actively police the information that comes into your life so that you can easily maintain a happier state.

To better use social media platforms like Facebook, all you need to do is be actively aware of how it is affecting you. If you know that seeing something on your feed will lead to negative emotions, then you don't have to see it. There is nothing wrong with putting your mental health first and deciding what is in your best interests. Be more responsible with your social media usage by monitoring the information that you see and immediately stopping things that you know won't make you feel happy.

There is no need to surround yourself by negativity when you know how it will make you feel. Furthermore, if it's the mere act of going on Facebook that's the problem, then you can fix this, too. If you find yourself constantly checking your phone for updates, or obsessing over what others are doing, you need to be aware of this and take a break. By filtering what you can see and realizing that you don't need to be constantly aware of everyone else's updates, you will better appreciate the world around you and the positivity that you have access to.

This is something that is relevant in real life as well. When speaking to someone about nothing but negative topics, it will be no surprise if you become turned off or want to leave the conversation early. Why would you intentionally surround yourself with things that don't make you happy? Everyone has enough problems and worries in their own lives without dealing with more. The only remedy is to surround yourself with positive things so that you will reciprocate the emotions that they provide.

This knowledge is not only useful to change how you interact with the world but can also help you in other ways. By these principles, if you want to be viewed positively, then you must make people associate you with positive things. This can be easily achieved if you speak only of uplifting things and stop getting caught up in the negatives.

There is so much of life to be positive about and so often we will only concentrate on what we do that's wrong. It's very refreshing to be faced with a positive attitude and people will immediately respond. Answer questions with positive stories or solutions, and if you're not fake or manipulative about it, then the other person's mood will also start lifting.

Because we love to spend time with people who make us happy, you will be instantly more likeable to whoever you are speaking to. Your positivity will rub off on them and soon you will be sharing happy things back and forth because you are both sharing your positive energy.

This isn't always easy. Some people can be intent on wallowing in their bad moods. A terrible day at work or a piece of bad news can mean that they might not be as receptive to your good mood as they otherwise would be. However, if you persist and keep talking about uplifting stories or experiences, you might just be able to life their spirits again. After all, everyone appreciates good news.

Being constantly surrounded by happiness and positive energy will eventually rub off on anyone. It's hard not to absorb something off that. This creates a chain effect where both of you will continue encouraging each other and you will eventually reach a stage of mutual comfort. They will now associate you with their current feeling of happiness, and this is a very powerful way to ensure likeability.

Keep in mind that your purpose is to increase mutual level of comfort. You need to make the first move, and don't expect the other person to be immediately receptive to your positivity. Be prepared for resistance and make sure you have an arsenal of positive stories or experiences, even if they're from friends or family.

Once you make another person reach that heightened level of enthusiasm, there's no telling where the conversation will go. You will be more likeable because you've helped increase their positivity, and you will both be rewarded by your mutual positivity. You'd be surprised by just how much injecting a high level of positivity and optimism into a conversation can liven up the exchange and leave a lasting impression on anyone.

Chapter 11. Social Efficiency (Who to Spend Time and Effort On)

Your social life is a big part of who you are and how you are seen. Some people seem to have dozens of friends and appear to make friends incredibly easily, while others seem to struggle in that department. So how do you go about improving your social life? It's easy enough to say that you need more friends and connections, but often, as hard as you may try, sometimes the friendships you pursue just don't work out.

Luckily, there is a way to focus your efforts so that you can achieve maximum results. Being selective in your social efforts is a key part of being successful in your social life and maximizing your likeability. Sometimes, despite putting all your energy into something, it can yield minimum results. To combat this, you need to know where to put your time, effort, and energy so that you don't waste resources on something that will never succeed.

Focus Your Firepower

How many friendships can you really have at one time? It's hard to keep up friendships, and often you may feel that you either have too few or too many. You may even feel like it's your fault if some don't work out, but the truth is that it's completely normal. Any relationship takes effort, but the important thing is to make sure the effort you put in will have the right rewards.

If you want to maximize your likeability, you need to think about the effort that you are putting in and how that translates in return. Return on effort really boils down to getting maximum results while putting in as minimum effort as possible. It's all about effective resource management. Your time, effort, and energy are finite resources. You need to guide them well. You don't want to find yourself in a situation where you're spreading out all these resources and getting very uneven results.

The way to do this is to stop wasting your time on people who will never reciprocate the time or effort that you put in. You need to know what you're aiming to get out of a relationship. Maybe it's a deep, close, personal connection, and you need to find someone who is willing to give you this. It's important for you to consider this because according to research in a British study, human beings can only have an average of three really close friends.

This study was conducted by Jari Saramäki, of the Aalto University School of Science in

Finland. The study recruited 24 students aged 17–19, with equal numbers of males and females. Each student was given an 18-month contract from a major mobile phone company and received 500 free monthly minutes and unlimited texts. In the beginning, the students were all located in the same city in the United Kingdom, but by the end, 10 had moved to universities in other parts of England.

Each student completed a questionnaire at the beginning, listing the names and numbers of their friends, work and school acquaintances, and known relatives. They then ranked those individuals on a scale of "emotional closeness" from 1 to 10, with 10 signifying someone "with whom you have a deeply personal relationship." They filled this questionnaire three times, at the beginning, the halfway mark, and the end.

Those who had been rated on the higher end of the scale also had high frequency and duration of phone calls, leading researchers to believe that it was a reasonable indicator of intimacy. The researchers created a ranking system for each contact based on frequency and call duration by analyzing the students' phone invoices.

It was discovered that although the students all had shifting friendships throughout the period, the number of people a person called and how long they spoke to them was consistent through the 18-month period. This meant that though a person's friendships changed, the intensity of those friendships was equal. For example, a person's top three contacts typically got 40–50% of the person's calls, even when those three changed over time.

This led to the conclusion that at any given time, we generally have three top friends. That's not to say that you don't care about any of your other friends or that you should cut them out of your life, but this research indicates that there are three people whom you involve in your life the most, based on the volume of minutes and the duration of calls they made. They won't always be the same people, as people often walk in and out of your life, but there will always be around three.

So what does this mean? Well, if you think about it, this isn't just relevant for figuring out who your friends are and whom you are closest to. It is also helpful knowledge when you consider the reverse situation. Which of your friends think that you are in their top three? And following on, do you have a chance of moving into the top three of anyone else?

These are important questions to ask when you are considering those who are important to you, and those whom you are important to. In terms of maximizing return effort, it is more useful and effective to focus your efforts on people whom you rank high for, instead of someone who doesn't even rank you in their top ten, or someone who will never include you in their top tier of friendship. You need to focus your firepower on those who will focus on you.

It's not a bad thing to admit that friendships are hard. They are. And they take lots of work between both parties. If you solidify your top three and focus your efforts on them, you will stop spreading your time, effort, and emotion. All of these things are valuable and need to be spent with care.

Don't be offended or saddened if someone leaves your top three. People are always going to have their own lives and own paths to take. If they have replaced you, soon enough, someone else will fill their place in your life as well. It's just nature and the way of life.

If you break it down in terms of resource management, you will find that it doesn't make sense to focus your time and effort on a relationship that is uneven from the start. If you know that you are the only one putting in the effort of calling, making plans, and meeting up, then it may be time to consider that you point your efforts elsewhere.

If the reverse is true, that you are making no effort while your friend carries the relationship, this is a strong sign that they will soon pull away. They can only have three close friends, and it is too much to ask that they waste their efforts on someone who will not return them.

When finding friends or trying to make someone into a top-tier friend, you need to gauge whether they are receptive to your efforts and whether it is likely they will return them in the future. If your effort seems to be paying off, then continue. However, if they aren't interested or if you feel your respective efforts are uneven, then you may need to find someone else. Again, this doesn't mean cutting them completely out of your life. It's okay when friends drift apart.

The core of the matter is that you need to value your time and effort. Respect yourself enough to realize that you need to get a good return for the time, attention, and emotion you're investing in people, or it just isn't fair to anyone. You don't need to spread yourself thin trying to make hundreds of friends and make sure that everyone likes you. You will end up disappointing everyone, including yourself. Instead, narrow down your friendships and focus on those that you know you will ultimately get the most reward from.

Being a Good Ally

What do you look for in your friends? Is it someone to keep you company, someone who shares interests with you and enjoys the same activities? It may very well be all of these things, but a study done by psychologists have concluded that we choose our friends based on an unconscious notion that they will support us in our times of need.

The study, performed by cognitive psychologists Peter DeScioli and Robert Kurzban, researched the cause of human friendships. The researchers asked the participants a number of questions where they ranked their closest friends in several ways, such as the benefits they receive from the friendship, the number of secrets shared, and how long the friendship had been ongoing.

The results concluded that people perceive their friendships as "deeper" depending on how they think that person can support them in potential conflicts. These can be trivial arguments to violent fights, or they can be on a more internal level such as supporting your path in life. So you are more likely to consider someone a good friend if they can do things for you, and bring some sort of value to the table in terms of conflict resolution, protection, or opening career doors.

This is also true for the reverse. If you don't think someone can do much for you or assist you in any way, then you will rank them lower, regardless of how well you get along or how great a time you have together. This is because you do not see them as someone who will be an ally in your time of need, when you face tough challenges or find yourself in physically dangerous situations.

From an evolutionary standpoint, it is not difficult to understand why we would do this. Thousands of years ago, life was very uncertain and this reflected in the way relationships were made and how people were valued. If you knew someone could protect you, tell you the best place to harvest plants, or the best way to hunt a large animal, they would be incredibly more important to you than the person who relied on you to show them things but gave nothing in return.

If certain people didn't have the built-in tendency to make allies, they tended not to pass on their genes. Why? Because they were less likely to survive, whether it was when they faced the next winter or were faced with predatory animals. It can be argued that our tendency to size people up based on how they can benefit us both as allies and as close friends is hardwired into our DNA. It just doesn't make sense to give someone your friendship while getting nothing in return.

But when we're thinking of our likeability and our modern friendships, how can this knowledge help? Though we are not cavemen anymore, we still retain that same mentality that we need people around us who can benefit our lives in some way. You can easily use this information to your advantage by proving to those around you that you bring something to the table, and will carry your own weight in the relationship. To make sure they know this, you need to communicate it, whether it is in a verbal or non-verbal way.

For example, in a networking environment, there's nothing wrong with telling people that you're connected to a big corporation or governmental structure that they can benefit from. You don't need to spell it out in an obvious way. That can seem cocky or arrogant. You just need to lay out the facts and let people reach their own conclusion that you can benefit and support them.

Maybe the benefit is in the form of a job. Maybe the benefit can even be somewhat intangible like social status. Whatever the case may be, when you make it clear to people that there is some sort or advantage to knowing you, they will be more likely to consider you an ally.

Once they believe this, you will instantly be more likeable, for the sole fact that they will believe that you are helpful and that you can offer them something others can't. It sounds very transactional, and maybe it is, but there's no denying that nobody wants or needs a friend who constantly needs support but gives none in return. You don't need to offer monetary gain; sometimes encouragement, humor, entertainment, or advice can work just as well.

Keep in mind that it is a thin tightrope between stating your potential value and just bragging about it. Nobody appreciates someone who overestimates their worth or just tries to show off. What is important is letting people know that you are willing to be on their side and help them in any number of ways, without trying to overstate your importance.

It isn't always about telling everyone that you have certain friends or a certain amount of money. Different people want different things and it is important to remember that just because someone may be interested in a career-related boost doesn't mean that another person is interested in the same. Maybe a person is more interested in personal development and needs someone to help them keep focus.

Sometimes you need to be strategic in targeting your friends. If you know that someone can offer you something that nobody else can, or if you know that you can have a mutually beneficial relationship with someone, approach them and see where it goes. The main aim is that the more useful you seem, the more likeable you are, and the more likeable you are, the more you can develop mutually beneficial relationships.

Being Selective

Being selective in your social efforts is about recognizing opportunities and knowing where your efforts would best be focused, and these are only a few suggestions that will help you do this. By following these ideas, you won't be wasting your time, effort, and energy, which are all valuable commodities. Instead, you will be maximizing your likeability by targeting your social efforts in a way that you know will lead to the best outcome.

Conclusion

It would be a lie if I said that on my way to adulthood, I had successfully eliminated all instances of the type of internal judgment from the introduction of this book.

But at least I'm aware, which is typically the toughest of tasks: *to think about your thinking*. Now, compound thinking about your thinking while you're in the heat of the moment with strangers, trying to make a good impression, and also trying to think of something witty to say.

That sentence probably made some of you sweat and cringe just reading it. But that's the reality of social intelligence, and any time you simply want to improve something about yourself. You have to begin by thinking about thinking until it becomes an instinct.

Otherwise, in the social context, you will be trying to hear the response from someone while trying to formulate a question in your head simultaneously. Your attention will be in two places, and that typically doesn't end well. That's where social intelligence begins - from feeling somewhat silly and stupid. But that's not where it will end with the knowledge in this book, and you know the real life benefits you can gain from it.

Sincerely,

Patrick King

Social Interaction Specialist and Conversation Coach at
www.PatrickKingConsulting.com

P.S. If you enjoyed this book, please don't be shy and drop me a line, leave a review, or both! I love reading feedback, and reviews are the lifeblood of Kindle books, so they are always welcome and greatly appreciated.

Speaking and Coaching

Imagine going far beyond the contents of this book and dramatically improving the way you interact with the world and the relationships you'll build.

Are you interested in contacting Patrick for:

- A social skills workshop for your workplace
- Speaking engagements on the power of conversation and charisma
- Personalized social skills and conversation coaching

Patrick speaks around the world to help people improve their lives through the power of building relationships with improved social skills. He is a recognized industry expert, bestselling author, and speaker.

To invite Patrick to speak at your next event or to inquire about coaching, get in touch directly through his website's contact form at http://www.PatrickKingConsulting.com/contact, or contact him directly at Patrick@patrickkingconsulting.com.

Cheat Sheet

Chapter 1.

It's in our DNA—humans are social animals and can literally decline in health without social interaction. We evolved to be able to socialize better, though there are limits to just how many people we can actually have relationships with.

Chapter 2.

Being popular and well-liked isn't necessarily a product of being witty and sharp. There are traditional markers, such as prestige and dominance, as well as subconscious ones such as sensitivity to popularity and being motivated by social interaction.

Chapter 3.

A habit more of us should indulge in is simply to shut up. Shut your mouth. Stop talking, especially when it's about you, your accomplishments, things that don't matter, and things that people haven't asked to hear.

Chapter 4.

Is it really this simple? Actually, yes. Emotional contagion is very real, and you can make others feel more positive and happy from your presence, which in addition makes them crave your presence.

Chapter 5.

The judgments we make are incredibly important to how others treat us—note that I said how others treat us. The gain-loss principle, Pygmalion Effect, and cognitive fluency theory are all ways that we unknowingly affect social interaction. Chapter 6.

It's so important there are two chapters about it. Reciprocity, self-verification, and in-group dynamics instantly create feelings of interest.

Chapter 7.

People are predictable in what they want, which is convenient. They crave social sharing to the same extent they crave sex and food, and they crave similarity.

Chapter 8.

Emotions are important yet ambiguous. Understanding them is key with concepts such as social calibration, reading fiction, emotional intelligence, and being the first to be vulnerable.

Chapter 9.

Sometimes, it just takes one negative trait to undo all of your other work and value. Emotional suppression, being too nice, and lacking eye contact are among the worst sins.

Chapter 10.

The world functions on the words of others out of convenience, and the word of mouth effect is powerful. Likewise, how people see and interact with you via social media can be equally as powerful.

Chapter 11.

You can't spend time with everyone, so you must be particular about whom you prioritize. Some people may become your allies, and some just might never enter your top three.

15.11.22